MY LITTLE TOWN

"'I don't hate [the South],' Quentin said, quickly, at once, immediately; 'I don't hate it,' he said. I dont hate it he thought, panting in the cold air, the iron New England dark: I dont. I dont! I dont hate it! I dont hate it!"

— WILLIAM FAULKNER, *Absalom, Absalom!*

"One place understood helps us understand all places better."

— EUDORA WELTY, *The Optimist's Daughter*

MY LITTLE TOWN

A Pilgrim's Portrait
of a
Uniquely Southern Place

D.B. TIPMORE

PHOTOGRAPHS BY
FRANK C. WILLIAMS

NEWSOUTH BOOKS

Montgomery

Newsouth Books
105 S. Court Street
Montgomery, AL 36104

Library of Congress Cataloging-in-Publication Data

Names: Tipmore, David, author.
Title: My little town: a pilgrim's portrait of a uniquely Southern place /
David Tipmore.
Description: Montgomery: NewSouth Books, [2020] | Includes
bibliographical references and index.
Identifiers: LCCN 2020032544 (print) | LCCN 2020032545 (ebook) | ISBN
9781588384331 (hardback) | ISBN 9781588384348 (epub)
Subjects: LCSH: Tipmore, David—Homes and haunts—Alabama—Marion.
| City and town life—Alabama—Marion. | Marion (Ala.)—History. |
Marion (Ala.)—Social conditions. | C (Ala.)—Race relations. | Marion
(Ala.)—Biography.
Classification: LCC F334.M37 T56 2020 (print) | LCC F334.M37 (ebook) |
DDC 976.1/44–dc23
LC record available at https://lccn.loc.gov/2020032544
LC ebook record available at https://lccn.loc.gov/2020032545

Design by Randall Williams
Printed in the United States of America by Sheridan

*The Black Belt, defined by its dark, rich soil, stretches across central
Alabama. It was the heart of the cotton belt. It was and is a place of great
beauty, of extreme wealth and grinding poverty, of pain and joy. Here we
take our stand, listening to the past, looking to the future.*

To my friends and family, for their support,
and to the citizens of Lovelady, for their inspiration.

CONTENTS

Author's Note

I have tried to recreate accurately events, locales, and conversations from my memory. I have changed the names of individuals and places to respect anonymity.

MY LITTLE TOWN

A Beginning

Our story begins happily enough. In 1860, a Southern planter decided to give his bride a wedding gift, a house which expressed the extravagance of his love and, more to the point, the vanity of a man who owned twenty thousand acres of arable land.

He went quickly to work on his dream, hiring a famous Philadelphia architect and overseeing the plans for an octagonal house of thirty-two thousand square feet, complete with five floors, a dome, twenty-six fireplaces, twenty-four built-in closets, four wine cellars, and eight bedrooms. By September of 1861, his slaves had completed the brickwork for the exterior patios and laid the cypress floors in the basement. They were beginning to apply the finishing plaster to the walls when they saw explosions on the horizon. The planter assured everyone they had nothing to fear, that his well-known anti-secession views and the Letter of Protection given him by Union General Ulysses S. Grant would keep the plantation intact and see the wedding gift through to completion.

This is a story about the Deep South, however, and its narrative turns on betrayal. The planter's assurances soon proved hollow. As the staircase to the second floor was being installed, fires from the burning cotton crop appeared in the distance, and the planter realized that General Grant's promise had gone up in smoke. Within a year, the plantation was destroyed, its crops and timber plundered, its farm machinery confiscated. The following year the planter died, pneumonia accomplishing what the war could not, and by 1864, nothing remained of his dream but an imposing five-story wooden frame and twelve tombstones in the nearby family plot.

If this tragedy had taken place in Connecticut, if less operatic versions were not so familiar to the histories of many Southern families, I would think the story irrelevant to present-day America and something of a twice-told tale. But tragedy, especially tragedy built on betrayal, bears bitter fruit for centuries. The sets of blood-soaked grievances—political and social, black and white, rural and urban—which lock the Deep South into a past squarely at odds with that of Kansas or Idaho or Maine, continue to remind the people who live here of the fraud inherent in much of what the rest of us tell ourselves about our national purpose.

Just for a moment, let us set aside blacks. (Just for a moment.) Can you imagine living among the ashes of the Confederacy in 1866? The humiliation fouled the air: to have to eat so much crow on such a grand scale, a historical scale, must have sickened the white natives of these states to a degree unimaginable north of the Mason-Dixon line. Why wouldn't their humiliation become intolerable? Why wouldn't it easily convert to anger? Of course, the resulting anger seemed rather toothless. At first. However, time worked its magic, as did schoolbooks written by the Daughters of the Confederacy, and the anger found an energy. It could be directed into a rationale! And how easily the rationale became a Cause, one which replaced humiliation and anger with a pride sourced in a rebellious (if hollow) righteousness. The Cause could reinterpret the bloodbath at Chickamauga into a glorious battle. The 25,000 Confederate bodies stinking on the fields of Gettysburg could vanish inside a heroic memory, perfumed with valor. And the Cause could sustain, propel its believers forward through time until the original humiliation was effectively obscured.

Long after 1865, many Southern whites (note the rather inadequate use of skin color to denote races in this book), are still embracing their humiliation, their Cause, are still holding tight to this idea of being tricked, fooled to a degree unlike any other cultural group in the rest of the country. Many of these Southerners still seek out convenient prisms to recast their difficult history. To listen to them talk about these grievances is to imagine yourself in conversation with Germans in the Weimar Republic after the signing of the Treaty of Versailles. Rationales and finger-pointing abound. You hear about the injustice of Reconstruction. You hear about Sally Hemings and Thomas Jefferson and the slave owners in the pre-Civil War Union states. You hear about the political calculation behind Abraham Lincoln's Emancipation Act of 1862. You hear about the "courageous" 2013 U.S. Supreme Court decision to invalidate key provisions of the Voting Rights Act of 1965. In 2021, you still hear about the "right" to secede. You hear about the injustice of Federal "interference" in all sorts of matters. You do not hear much about the system of slavery and its long-standing benefits to a certain group, *their group*, except in the few seconds of conversation needed to switch the topic.

As you listen, you can hear (and actually feel) that many of these white Southerners think of themselves as outcasts, viewed with pity, hatred, or distaste by a nation whose economic concerns and global engagement and sense of modernity have passed them by. They seem to be watching, fuming, as their industries are outsourced, their religions mocked, their way of life reduced to the plot of a situation comedy, their totems—all those Confederate statues!—removed by high-handed fiats.

Considering this perspective, why wouldn't they—the defiant Scots and Irish who settled this region—create their own culture, live by their own values, *prefer Judge Roy Moore?* Proudly and angrily, they vote as a separate country, educate their children through an ugly clash of public and private schools, devise their own religious denominations, imagine their own fiction, speak their own language, believe their own *facts*—and all with an intense conformity that is as much a given within the region as it is anathema outside it.

Their anger is not without a formidable companion. The historic anger of these white Southerners, so fueled by guilt and shame, is shadowed by the equally historic anger of many black Southerners. *Their* anger, fueled by a righteous entitlement, defines their present just as it determined their past. Many blacks can still barely see over the historical wall of oppression which they have sought to tear down for decades. They find it difficult to discuss issues of race with many white Southerners especially because they believe the racism continues, albeit more skillfully hidden. They can barely speak intimately about it, preferring to turn their anger into buildings (and monuments) reflecting their position, as can be seen in the harsh assessment of their long suffering exhibited in the Legacy Museum in Montgomery, Alabama.

And, they would argue, why do they need to explain themselves or their injurious history, yet again? Why *should* they feel obliged to try and understand, let alone befriend, the descendants of people who beat them, lynched them, sold them, cheated them, hunted them down, denied them the vote, kept them in figurative chains for decades after their emancipation? These same people are doing it now through sly evasions of covert racism and a criminal "justice" system determined to treat them as a special class. Forgiveness, be damned!

So the dramatic conflict lives on, underscores social gatherings, church events, political meetings: parallel angers, equally historic, equally surfeited with self-justification, equally skewed by an eternal victimhood. And equally responsible for creating a magnificent and singular drama, still being played out on the idiosyncratic stage of what is likely the last indigenous regional culture within the continental United States. Here in the Deep South, especially the rural Deep South, you live within a royal flush of peculiarities—divided societies, vanquished ancestors, Biblical zealotry, agrarian passions, paralyzed economies—that seem to have stalled the passage of time experienced by the rest of the nation. As such, the culture of the rural Deep South demands its own logic, provokes its own questions. Can it survive? Should it survive? Or will it finally give way to the inexorable assimilation into the larger frame of reference that now dominates the rest of America?

These questions beg another. Because of its singularity, could there be a place within our national borders more susceptible, more *fascinating*, to the interpretation of outsiders? Apparently not, as esteemed writers such as Alexis de Tocqueville and V. S. Naipaul and Paul Theroux have wandered through the area, creating their own reconstructions of it, maybe taking a trip through Mississippi or Alabama, maybe buying a house and living among the natives for a year, poking around just enough to get a "feel" for the *mise* of the local *scene* before publishing a book whose degree of authority is just sufficient to anger the few locals who read it.

And the reconstructions of these visitors beg yet one more question, a personal question. Can a damned Yankee, that is, a Yankee who has lived for more than a decade in a little town in the Black Belt of Alabama, ever really understand where he is living?

That is the answer I am searching for.

In so doing, I have tried to avoid the cursory judgments made by so many writers in the South living as if they were colonials in a distant land. I am attempting to master a perceptual tango that requires fancy footwork. I watch for a tendency to deceive myself that any sort of exposure to this culture allows me to play Margaret Mead to the local natives' Samoans. I work hard at maintaining a balance, struggle for objectivity. And I don't always succeed. Although I now take in stride news that a five-point buck has jumped through the display window of the local department store or listen calmly to a neighbor's story about the latest family feud, waged with mops and golf clubs, on the courthouse square, I am still taken aback when a county commissioner addresses a local activist as a "hanky-headed nigger." And I can still lose my critical bearings within the region's soft blanket of doom: the azaleas blooming among the ruins, the poverty so fierce it attains its own integrity, the historical rot so entrenched that understanding it is possible, according to William Faulkner, only by birthright.

Watching my efforts, the natives in my little town cut me some slack, shaking their heads at my silly attitude about guns, my laughable accent, my ignorance of so much of what they see as common sense. But we, the natives and I, keep adjusting our senses of rhythm. We hold each other within our dance's rigid and awkward embrace, learning which assumptions are wrong-footed, which prejudices to lean into, and, in the process, creating the oddest of odd couples, each party dependent on—and suspicious of—the other.

Home

A few facts about where I find myself.

Huntley County, Alabama: a predictable entry on any list of the poorest counties in America, where forty-seven percent of the residents live below the poverty line, where the average annual income is fifteen thousand dollars, where twenty percent of the residents are uninsured, where whites find themselves an unhappy minority.

Huntley County: described on National Public Radio with that degree of ignorance only a "coastal elitist" could achieve. ("People don't realize that places like Huntley County still exist," went the NPR teaser for a story about the horrors of our rural health care.)

Huntley County: at the heart of the heart of the Alabama Black Belt, a ribbon of seventeen counties decorating the central section of the state, counties where Walker Evans once wandered and photographed the sharecroppers for James Agee's *Let Us Now Praise Famous Men.*

Huntley County: home to Lovelady, my little town, birthplace of "Got A Date With An Angel" composer Hal Kemp, civil rights heroine Coretta Scott King, Stars and Bars designer Nicola Marschall, and Jimmie Lee Jackson, mortally shot by an Alabama state trooper while trying to protect his mother during a 1965 civil rights demonstration, an event which led directly to the famous march to Montgomery from nearby Selma.

And Lovelady: "The College City," three thousand citizens nestled around a Baptist women's college and a military institute, both in business since before the Civil War.

Rather, the War Between the States.

Rather, more to the local point, the War of Northern Aggression, a phrase I first heard uttered with just the gentlest touch of sarcasm by one of the local timber barons.

The War of Northern Aggression. There it was! Inside those words hid one of the unsettling moments I feel regularly when living in my little town. These moments follow no rules. Just when everything around me seems perfectly comprehensible, one of these moments, drone-like in its stealth, hones in on an unsuspecting presumption and blows it up.

Another moment, one that occurred during a breakfast conversation with a friend who was complaining about the injuries her son had suffered during a high school football game:

"Why doesn't he play soccer instead?" I offered.

The woman shot me a disapproving glance. "Soccer," she emphasized sternly, "is a Communist sport."

Yet another moment, occurring at a pancake supper at a local church:

"I don't understand why there aren't more black people here," I remarked to the church's pastor and his wife.

"Well, we always invite them, but they just don't seem to want to participate," he replied. "They have their own ways, after all."

A final example:

"Do you have a church?"

The woman posed the question to me in the manner of someone who had asked it many times before. I hesitated. Part of my confusion was the connotative twist on the verb: the idea of "owning" or "having" a church. The remaining confusion resulted from the question's purpose.

Was it a test of character? (*Of course it was. "Without" a church, you hardly exist in my little town.*)

Was it a query about my social class? (*Certainly. Had I answered "Baptist" or even "Methodist," the conversation would have been altered significantly. Had I answered "Unitarian" or "Catholic," the conversation would have ended.*)

Was it an expression of hospitality? (*Perhaps. And perhaps not. Behind the warm smile which accompanied the question lay a fierce, and sometimes unfriendly, competition to snare new members for a particular congregation.*)

"You're in and out in forty-five minutes," the woman added, describing her Sunday morning service. "It's the perfect fit for you."

An adept salesperson, she was sizing up her customer. And, up to a point, she was correct. I was, indeed, looking for a perfect fit, just not that particular kind. My "fit" had a more existential purpose: not only to understand my little town but to assimilate into it, to find a home for my wandering self, to make the years here mean something beyond an exercise in ethnography.

This struggle, my peculiar *Mein Kampf*, is the subplot of this book and, at the same time, its emotional center. On dispiriting midwinter afternoons, looking out my kitchen window across the grays and browns of the back lawn toward the stillness of Smith Street, I imagine myself a sentry in a new diaspora, a lonely scout for an army of men and women who, in their youth, fled inhospitable towns for what they thought were coastal dreamlands and who are now returning to what they imagine to be a quiet refuge.

I feel in good company with these people, fictional and real, comfortable among the famous American literary characters and American artists who lost and found themselves in what they saw as the more enticing possibilities of Elsewhere: Nick Carraway and Scott Fitzgerald, Holly Golightly and Truman Capote, Tennessee Williams and Willie Morris, Flannery O'Conner's Asbury Fox and William Faulkner's Quentin Compson, those many characters of Sinclair Lewis and Theodore Dreiser and Willa Cather, so many other dreamers of dreams impossible to pursue in St. Louis or Memphis or Jackson. Now, older, perhaps wiser, they—I—were drifting back from the siren songs of San Francisco and Boston, Los Angeles, and New York, back into the area of the country they—I—once dismissed as hostile, ignorant, unworthy.

But I was not going home again. I was going to a place that would put special demands on my gambit, requiring answers to strange questions. Could a worldly, irreverent, but *game* loner find a home in a town so opposite from his desires and experience? Would my experiment turn out to be a rehash of a Hallmark television movie, the jaded urbanite finding redemption among the country folk? Or, even worse, would my adventure freeze into the cold musings of a *flaneur*, careful observations reducing the people around me to curiosities?

Chances seemed about even. I wasn't without some of the skills reportedly requisite for living in a tiny town in the Deep South. I could make a decent side dish for a potluck supper. I could keep a presentable home and a passable lawn. I could even operate a Bush Hog. But could I assume the social rhythms? Could I quietly accept the intensely held political and religious opinions? Could I master the conversational *rebop* so peculiar to the Deep South? Could, ultimately, a pearl appear from all the grains of sand inside this odd little oyster?

We shall see.

A Tour

Welcome to Lovelady, my little town.

First, a tour.

Grab one of those cardboard hand fans, with the picture of Jesus and the Baptist Church, for sale outside the "black" barber shop. You'll need it. It's August, the dry season. A hot breeze rustles the leaves of the pecan and magnolia trees. The air is heavy with a scrim of red dust. The grass, brown and thin and barely covering the clay soil, died many weeks ago.

But have faith. Keep driving into town on County Road 301, from the south. The outskirts float into view, a miasma of buildings almost willfully bereft of appeal: a rural health center, the headquarters of the Highway Department, a Dollar General store, a Family Dollar store, a few pillared antebellum mansions whose poetic names ("Quietude," "Resolute") are announced on hand-painted signs.

County Road 301 blends into Pickett Street, the main street of my little town. Crossing a small bridge over some railroad tracks, you look over and see a nearly empty 1970s-style shopping plaza, its storefronts facing the Hilltop Minimart, a half-hearted competitor that somehow outlasted the shuttered Hardee's across the street.

You pass a parade field. In the distance are tennis courts, a quadrangle surrounded by handsome brick buildings, a chapel worthy of an English village: the campus of Lovelady's military institute, one of the oldest of its kind in the United States. An even more haphazard stretch of Pickett Street follows, throwing together parsonages (Presbyterian, Methodist), "black" and "white" Baptist churches, a small bank, a grand home or two, a defunct filling station or two, more mini-marts, a forgotten utilities office. You see a swimming pool. Stop for a moment and consider its prominent placement in the town. Wonder why it is now so derelict, deserted.

And across the street from the swimming pool? A forest of magnolias, the huge, historic kind of tree on which in the spring shiny blossoms cover the thick green leaves with bursts of white. This forest of magnolias obscures a historic home: the Boswell House, pillared, porched, grand as only my little town was once grand, a house of thousands of square feet of antiquity now rotting from neglect. Consider this house an object lesson of sorts, a silent sermon on the passage of time and on the consequences of failing to meet the stern demands of properties built on a scale and for a way of life no longer plausible.

But move on, move on, past the brick beauty of Rinehart College, one of the last Baptist women's colleges in the United States. Say hello to the town square, its two-story brick storefronts painted, if at all, in safe, economical colors: taupes, faded olives. Notice the ghosts of prosperous pasts—the names of Jewish merchants inlaid in the tiled floors of the entrances, the comparative grandeur of the old bank (now empty), the magnificent 1832 courthouse. Admire the

plantings around the courthouse; understand how even something this simple inspired those intricate controversies so customary to small towns. In this case, the civic dialogue crackled for at least a few months with crabby accusations:

Do not touch the aging pecan trees on the courthouse lawn.

But they are scraggly and past their prime. They need to go. We will plant other trees.

But no one will water them.

Then let us plant flowers.

No flowers! They will die in the heat.

But we need some color.

Color costs money. Are you going to pay for it?

Back and forth, forth and back, disputes about the landscaping careening in all directions, in editorials, in gossip, in friendships rent down the middle from side-taking.

There is more to say about the Court House and its civic implications: the financial questions raised by the installation of its elevators; the rationale behind the levies charged for auto tags; the puzzling system of project bidding; the lopsided racial composition of the County's public sector employees.

However, let it be for the moment. Move on. Glance further around the square and see how incompletely the few architectural successes disguise the no-frills needs of the businesses: a discount store, an abandoned clothing store, an abandoned child care center, a drug store, two 1970s-era civic buildings which constitute City Hall and the Fire Department.

Then continue down Pickett Street, past the square, staring into the blackness of empty, but once attractive, display windows. Wish these windows well; they have housed a succession of dreams, dreams that exhausted thousands of dollars, dreams born of enthusiasms materializing as dress shops or toy stores, dreams that appeared and then as suddenly disappeared in the exhaust fumes of a truck, the owner leaving behind a foreclosure or an unpaid rent check. Dashed dreams, a reminder of failures and plans gone awry. My little town specializes in them.

But enough of all that sadness. See on down Pickett Street, a little further? Lift your spirits by waving to cheery Ned Grissom, manager of Grissom & Banks, an antiques mall converted from the old Beall Hardware Store. Antiques stores are common to the area around my little town; they provide tangible, convenient access to the grandness of the past.

As is often the case, Ned is smoking a cigarette, sitting on one of the for-sale chairs lined up on the sidewalk in front of the store. Ned is a practiced charmer, a natural salesman. He maintains a canny closeness with many of the prominent matrons of my little town, who often use his establishment to shop for birthday gifts and hostess favors. In something so redolent of "atmosphere" that you might think it inspired by a movie set, an old dining table near the store's entrance serves as a local watering hole. Around the table, perhaps eating a take-out hamburger or sipping a cup of coffee from Mama's Restaurant, you will find the most vivid local expression of "diversity": matrons of the highest order, drifters who help customers load antiques onto their trucks, august town historians, estate auctioneers, Rinehart College professors looking for chat, tennis coaches, loyal out-of-town customers.

The local bachelors, me among them, visit the store in the fervid manner of Egyptologists returning to Luxor, hopeful for some new discovery: a Tiffany lamp, a tester bed, an oriental rug *that is not machine-made*. Ned is happy to take customers on a guided tour through the vendors' stalls, quick to seize on even the slightest enthusiasm and bend it into exactly what the unsuspecting didn't realize they were looking for.

And then, across the street, see the proud, handsome brick library, a story in itself, wrestled from the brink of crumbling irrelevance and reinvented by the diligence of one of the town's leading ladies into an attractive, well-staffed asset; pretty, yes, yet an asset whose books remain largely untouched.

Pause for a moment. Beside the library sits an open-air gazebo, useless except for events in the late fall and late spring, the few weeks when the weather allows for standing under the turreted roof, having a glass of scuppernong wine or a tiny pimento cheese sandwich or one of Mr. Nielsen's revered sugar cookies. For what purpose was this building erected? The answer lies somewhere among the ravages of the town's racial divide; construction of the pretty gazebo holds some of the ugliest suspicions each of my little town's races harbors about the other, as they battle over where to spend our meager financial resources.

My little town's races. The phrase reverberates with a need for clarification, resistances felt rarely in the outside world (or ninety miles away, for that matter). Although blacks dominate whites two to one, walking around the square might lead you to assume otherwise. Rather than flaunt their majority, the black citizens seem to hang around the edges of town life: a bank teller here, a florist there, a waitress, a postmistress, some sanitation workers roaring by on a truck. These men and women don't behave as if they're in the majority. They don't walk down the street with a sense of privilege or command. Their eyes seem to avoid yours; often, they look down at the sidewalk when they walk by, as if they were searching for secure footing. (At four-way stops, they often accede all too readily to any white driver, causing a frustrating game of who-shall-go-first.) A paralyzing politeness seems to rule many attempts at outreach by either race, a caution, an acquiescence, haunted by the ghosts of past roles. The men will say "All *right!*" to many of the salutations you send their way, sometimes creating a *non sequitur* in response to a query about the weather or a question about health. This rejoinder, usually delivered with a heartiness that cannot possibly be sincere, remains one of the most effective ways of ending a conversation I have ever encountered.

Us and them. As you walk farther around the square, you cannot escape observing the two races sliding by each other, much as different castes pass on the streets of Mumbai. And why shouldn't they? These people don't really know you, nor you them. Your lives only glance against each other, skirt around each other. You don't go to church with them. You don't often eat with them. You don't get your hair cut with them. You don't talk with them about much besides football and barbecue. They frequent their own shops, buy their own hair products. The "black" package store down the hill, the "Stop and Stab" convenience store (which, in a most poignant case of stereotyping, has the best fried chicken in town), the black daycare center, the black optician, all drift in the background of a downtown dominated by white-owned banks, white-owned pharmacies, white-owned florists, white-owned antique stores, white businesses everywhere, making any transactions with blacks—the race that actually governs the town through their majorities on the City Council and County Commission—formulaic, frustrating, and ultimately futile.

And so a desire for a greater presence of blacks on our tour, or in my life in Lovelady, remains a fool's errand, a notion so reflective of an optimistic autosuggestion that it can only come from someone unfamiliar with the cemented social construct of almost any small town in the Deep South. The emblematic lunch counters of the 1950s may now be officially integrated, but find one where you can see the two races enjoying a relaxed harmony. Too much has happened. Too few common interests can be found. The past casts too long a shadow. New generations must emerge for the long-awaited communion to occur.

Our tour is almost finished. But keep going down Pickett Street. At the far end you'll see two of the pillars of religious life in my little town: The United Methodist Church (the one with the notable steeple) and the beautiful 1838 jewel box of an Episcopal Church (the one with the notable cemetery). These two churches, together with the First Baptist Church, serve the town's professional class and help maintain the social order, an order that keeps the two colleges functioning, if not always awash in money or students.

I can see you need to sit down. Walking anywhere in August is

tantamount to Englishmen playing cricket in the noonday sun. And we've covered almost all of our downtown, or at least a suggestion of the spine of the town's skeleton. Mention should be made, however, of the section of Lovelady on the west side of Pickett Street. Between the military institute and Rinehart College lies the leafy swank of the Historic District, designated so by the National Register of Historic Places. The portals at the entrances to this District are not visible, but they exist virtually, even spiritually, in the sense that a home on Arbuthnot Street or West Howell or Lee lends to its owners that peculiar, almost supernatural, cachet attached to owners of "grand" homes anywhere.

And some of the homes are, indeed, grand; their over-sized formal salons and parlors and butler pantries and multiple porches are adorned with detailed woodwork and elaborate wainscoting and fourteen-feet-high ceilings that make a mockery of the supposedly luxe sales points of modern homes, all polystyrene crown molding and faux granite countertops fresh from Home Depot.

Appropriately, the lawns of homes in the Historic District demand—and usually receive—an attention reserved for public gardens. In the hot mornings of the late spring months, the silky air is shattered by the sounds of weed eaters and leaf blowers and zero-turn riding mowers. Owners of the homes swear by their particular "lawn man" with the same fervor the Renaissance Popes vouched for their personal painters and sculptors.

Mr. Thomas mows the lawn at my house on Lee Street, mows it with a reverence that allows him to create lines in the grass as precise as corn rows, elaeagnus bushes as tailored as a Galanos suit, sidewalks as edged as the sugar flowers on a wedding cake. "Mr. Thomas," I call him; he calls me "Mr. David." That we have established an understanding across race and class stirs a certain mistrust among some of the natives of my little town. This mistrust may have to do with the suspicion that I overpay him or may have to do with my being an outsider whose ancestors had a less explicit involvement with slavery.

"You let him work in your home *when you're not there?*" is a question I often hear from my friends and neighbors. Yes, I answer them, and go one step further: I even allow Thomas to use the guest bathroom.

Toward the western end of Lee Street, you can take a left turn and suddenly find yourself in "The Hill," the slum of my little town, a lost world of government checks and stabbings and upholstered sofas on porches. The poverty of the district, however, is belied by the showroom-fresh BMWs and Corvettes roaring past my house toward this destination. They might lead you to infer that a special inducement lies at the end of this particular rainbow, some pot held precious in local eyes.

This inference would be true; the Hill is the home of much of the drug peddling in my little town. Cadets from the military institute eager for off-limits hijinks occasionally find themselves being guided into the back seat of a police car after an ill-conceived attempt to buy marijuana or salvia, our local version. Long-held feuds among the African American families occasionally end in a knife fight and a headline in the *Times-Standard*.

The saddest irony about the location of The Hill concerns its immediate proximity to Lincoln Normal School, founded in 1867 by freed slaves as an attempt to formalize public education for their children. Here, in this low, red brick structure, Coretta Scott King and civil rights activists Edythe Scott Bagley and Jean Childs (the wife of Andrew Young) once took geometry tests, flirted, and ate lemon icebox pie in the cafeteria, enjoying a modest youth before their exceptional destinies caught up with them.

In all other directions, my little town fades into a countryside of low hills, double-wide trailers, fields of corn, cotton, and soybeans, woods of oak and pecan trees. Even Pecan Drive, a street of one-story "common" brick homes that passes for the suburbs of my little town, fritters unremarkably into the surrounding void just past Lovelady Academy, the private "Christian" (i.e., "white") school. Walking out beyond the Academy's forlorn football field, into the gullies and pastures of the countryside, you may be overwhelmed by a slightly humbler version of the feeling Wordsworth experienced while surveying the vistas of the Lake District above Tintern Abbey.

If, that is, you were of a poetic, and less grandiose, turn of mind. If you were not, you would merely feel the emptiness, the silence, the heat, accompanied by the buzzing of a thousand crickets, and wonder where in God's name you were. And why.

Why

Why, indeed?

Why would I, someone so literally estranged from such a place, end up where I was once introduced at an event (admittedly, with some humor) as "a participant in a federal witness protection program"?

The answer takes some explaining. I need to go back in time. For a few early years, formative years, I lived on a small farm. Among its unassuming hills and open skies, I first understood the power of nature unencumbered by the glare of city lights or echoes of traffic noise. As I wandered over the farm's hilly acres, investigating rock piles and the ditches along country roads, I realized that *no one in the world knew exactly where I was at that moment. I was alone. And untouchable.*

"There is pleasure in the pathless woods," wrote Lord Byron, echoing a host of Romantic poets who also craved this peculiar state of mind. "There is rapture in the lonely shore, there is society where none intrudes, by the deep sea, and music in its roar . . ." Of course my idea of "rapture" was juvenile, uninformed by literary context or historical comparison. At that age, I could feel only the joy, the deep aloneness, in those moments, knew that through them I could summon a bliss at once exotic and addictive.

The addiction never left me, not living in Philadelphia, or Manhattan, or Boston, or Miami, or Tangier, or Paris, or London. The further I moved away from it, the more a longing to experience the strange childhood ecstasy—and the memory of it—gripped me. Suddenly, I could no longer live as I had been living for decades, felt I had been too long in the most calculated versions of nature: flowers in pots, skies framed by apartment balconies. In my new little town, in the middle of a county whose density matched that of western North Dakota, I hoped to again lose, and perhaps gain, myself. I also hoped, more naively, that I might be able to again experience that same wonder about life I had known so little of for so long, but that is another story.

Can you see how this wish to "go home again" was predicated on a hunger for authenticity? Among the rural folk, follows this magical thinking, lies veracity. Among the simple people, with their unpolished accents and perspective unsullied by irony, lies peace. In this thinking, Patagonia is more "real" than Paris, the Empty Quarter *non pareil* in its purity of instinct.

And so I wandered through the world, often blindly, toward my impossibly idealized El Dorado, much as Van Gogh, smitten by a nostalgia for what he perceived as the "honesty" of the peasants working in the potato fields, once fled Paris for the countryside near Arles. And yet. I wish I had been unaware, as I wandered, that behind this urge lay a touristic impulse which rendered my efforts less than authentic, something with quotation marks around them.

Even while landing at the airports in Dubai or Caracas, I knew I had become locked in a disgusting, colonialist perspective: the constant traveler, after all, cannot ever be a native. He can only consume the authenticity of others.

Of course, I was always able to find a rationale for my restlessness. Who could blame me for wanting to escape those decades in the world's most sophisticated cities, forcing upon me their intense conformity, their obsession with the *au courant*. And so I would move on, never fully engaged with my surroundings, looking for something I remembered, vaguely, from an earlier life, an earlier *me*.

Would I finally locate that self here? It was a riddle within a quandary, a gamble whose odds were about even. Could I survive in a place dependent on the need to serve on a vestry? Could I risk disagreement, and possible banishment, from all my former city friends, with whom conversation would usually stop when they asked where I was living?

You live where?

So be it, I said, as I drove into the driveway of my Lovelady home for the first time. If this little town were to be my destiny, then I would make it fit, make it work for me. Where better to land than this sweet, tiny island of quiet, waiting so patiently for a visitor from another world who would touch down and learn about it and, perhaps, a little about himself?

History

I should give you a brief history of my little town. I don't really want to, and you'll probably skip it anyway, but I *should* because history is so much a part of the local milieu. Nowhere in the United States, New England notwithstanding, has history had such a distinctly *emotional* effect on a section of the nation.

And my little town is all about history *as emotion*. This is not to say that we do not have a strong sense of chronology. We have at least three dutiful, plodding chronological histories, most notably the two thick volumes by a local historian. These volumes, replete with dates and then-this-happened lists, capture the chronology of Lovelady, a narrative apparently patterned on an ever-shrinking vortex, the town getting smaller and smaller, circling down a drain until it seems to disappear.

So can I, should I, ignore Lovelady's brief years as a long-ago leading city of Alabama, one with almost thirty thousand residents? Or its lucky break during the Civil War, when the Union Army swept past the town in its rush to demolish the munitions factories in nearby Selma? Or its days as Queen of the Black Belt, where the soil is so dark and rich that the cotton fields once seemed an inexhaustible source of money and power, producing thousands of bales and sending them down the Alabama River to the port of Mobile?

Skip the history? Why not? Chronology of the past is so tedious, isn't it, so unrewarding to anyone bent on a more modernist perspective? Chronology is so *factual*, and facts do not permit enough grief and bitterness and romance and loss to satisfy either my purposes or that of many residents of my little town.

William Faulkner understood this idea most clearly. In Faulkner you find the most articulate vision of the hideous paradox of the history of my little town—to be eternally consumed by and yet sickened by its past. *The past as a wound* was the metaphor V. S. Naipaul used to describe the history of the Deep South. Or, to extend this metaphor, a wound so perpetually fresh that, with each scrape of the skin (any sort of federal intervention, any sort of imposition of modernity) out seeps some bloody recrimination.

And indeed the wound of Southern history, its immovable past refusing to let go of the present, runs deep through my little town, spreading throughout its tangible history (all the museums) to its architectural history (all the antebellum antiques) to its mercantile history (all the defunct family stores) to its religious history (all the historic churches). So much history to feel—and everywhere you look! All the plaques. All the pilgrimages. All the antebellum homes and landmarks and cemeteries dotted with graves marked with plastic bouquets and memorials to the Confederate Dead. Each street seems to bear the weight of a historical figure (Coretta Scott King, Jefferson Davis, Jimmie Lee Jackson) or of a crumbling building my little town can no longer afford to maintain. Each month seems to host an event designed to commemorate someone known for something which happened so long ago that only the most elderly remember it.

Can this past of my little town be sanctified? Can it be seductive? Yes, to both questions. Remember William Alexander Percy, Walker's adopted father and author of the controversial *Lanterns on the Levee*, in which he expressed many notorious opinions about "the Negro"? Think of the rich nostalgia of his poem "Home," its appreciation for the three staples that create the uniqueness of my little town: faith, farm, friendship.

> *. . . But I oh, I must go*
> *Back where the breakers of deep sunlight roll*
> *Across flat fields that love and touch the sky;*
> *Back to the more of earth, the less of man,*
> *Where there is still a plain simplicity,*
> *And friendship, poor in everything but love,*
> *And faith, unwise, unquestioned, but a star . . .*

Notice the reverence for simplicity, for the prosaic, for "unwise" faith. And, in this context, recall one of Percy's later more colorful references to what he feared would be the South's ultimate fate: its agrarian charms immolated by that "sideshow Götterdämmerung" represented by the rest of charmless, mercantilist America.

Little chance of that trend occurring in my little town, so remote, so economically downtrodden, so fierce in its battle against

the larger world of chain stores (with one revealing exception) and "unbiblical" churches and foreign languages, so fearful of a culture trying to push via freeways and airlines into our beloved hunting grounds of swamps and low hills and dense forests.

Given enough entropy and inertia, however, the citizens of my little town seem willing to allow its more negotiable bits of history to vanish. Do we miss the movie theater in my little town, gone twenty-five years? Yes, but not enough to revive it. Could we bring back Dozier's Hardware? Mickleboro's Jewelers? Well, we could, if only some fool would put up the money, have the energy, want to invest. Should we worry about our pockmarked streets, our shabby stately homes? Can someone please bring back the old hotel on the square, so much a part of scenes in the film version of Carson McCullers's *The Heart Is a Lonely Hunter*?

The answer, emphatically, lies in the shrinking population, and the school closures, and the shuttering of the power company headquarters. The hotel is not coming back, nor is the movie theater or jewelry store, nor those merchants. And so we sit as the past sneaks up on us, accumulating as quickly as the future disappears, misting my little town with a *pentimento* of memory and imagination.

Decay

How can I let you know how *much* I don't want to say it? How much it makes me sick to say it?

My little town is dying.

There. I've said it. But let's modify that statement. Let's say: my little town is struggling. It's trying to save itself. From itself.

We who live here only pretend to acknowledge this truth. Most of us avoid the subject or approach it with elaborate rationales or, among the more enterprising, devise *ad hoc* strategies to secure a better future, such as instituting a charter school or waging a campaign to reinvent the downtown square.

So, rather than "dying," or "struggling," let's put it another way: my little town is in the process of decay, from a fear of modernity, from addiction to the past, from fear of the future, from the disappearance of resources.

Who can mistake the signals: the preponderance of consignment shops, full of old trophies and other tired dreams; the rusted For Sale signs advertising—for months—the lovely, empty homes; the library open only one or two days a week. Some people in my little town are alarmed by these signals. Others are resigned to them. Still others (those who have the luxury of periodic escapes) seem to overlook them.

But overlooking the decay as you drive around or listen to one of the civic stalwarts takes a capacity for happy endings shared by only a few. Nightlife, family diversions in their most modest forms, exist only in memory. A bowling alley? Long gone. A video arcade? Unimaginable. A tavern? Closed. A movie theater? Once upon a time. A shopping center? Two, both half empty. Sporting events? Well, yes, if you count high school football games and the annual June rodeo.

And how quickly the pace of this decay is accelerating! Look! The old Waldrop home is for sale. And when did the Stewart building go on the block? And that vacant lot? And *that* building. And there's another house for sale. And another. Why is no one mowing the lawn at that house? *Because the Sherwoods moved away, to the coast.* And when did the five-and-dime close? What happened to the little cafe, the nail salon, the Chamber of Commerce? Civic life disappears so quickly in my little town, once the game is up.

Difficult question: When did my little town begin to decay? Easier question: when was my little town at its zenith? Some residents, such as Mr. Edward Nielsen, beloved high school instructor, remember bustling downtown streets on Saturdays in the 1950s, when the Pan Am Restaurant was in flower. Dr. James Polk, deceased curator of the county Preservation and Historical Society Museum, would have shown you photos from even earlier periods, pictures taken during the swing from the nineteenth into the twentieth century, of prosperous merchants in front of their dry goods stores, their law firms, their doctors' offices.

When did all this prosperity, these merchants and doctors and lawyers who built the grand homes in the Historic District, disappear? Here is where the answers contradict themselves depending on the age and authority of the speaker. Some older residents point to the boll weevil, eating its way through Southern cotton estimated to be worth billions of twenty-first-century dollars.

Others (especially the more rural residents) mention the crash of cotton prices after the Great War. Tellingly, few references are made of the dramatic loss of talent and manpower represented by the Great Migration, when almost six million blacks fled the area's Jim Crow laws and farm failures for what they hoped were better wages and living conditions and civic equality—and fewer lynchings. The omission of the Migration speaks directly to who is in charge of writing the history of the region. Or the Great Depression in 1929, when the South saw a violent free fall of bank failures and farm foreclosures, families abandoning homes they had occupied for three and four generations. Or the mid-1960s and the passing of civil rights legislation, when the segregated education and political systems were so abruptly shattered, and cultures, understood by each other for centuries through contradictory optics, were forced to live in a degree of proximity that quickly caused them to realize they had almost nothing in common.

But how pointless these explanations seem now, when my little town has only:

one drugstore

one dry cleaners
one "supermarket"
one doctor
one dentist
one hardware store
one real estate agent
two lawyers
one fast-food restaurant chain
and:
no clothing stores
no specialty medical practices (except, tellingly, a dialysis center)
no hospital
no local ambulance service
no jewelry store
no carwash
no chain stores (save Dollar General and Family Dollar)
no . . .

Lately, one breakfast-and-lunch cafe, the kind often seen in most media reproductions of small-town America, has appeared at the end of a defunct shopping center. And the cafe's success may actually be holding. Note, however, how deeply the racial divide extends, even into food. Very few blacks support this restaurant, an attitude which obeys the historical racial patterns. The whites in my little town have tried, and tried again, to keep just this sort of place in operation on the downtown square for many years. But there don't seem to be enough of them. I can't remember all the reincarnations of this restaurant, or that cafe, or bistro, each rolled out with fanfare, rolled out in the same location, as the owners redecorated the same storefront, posted a new menu outside the same front door, stood cheerfully by the cash register, hopes floating until someone died, or they couldn't get any help, or their few customers had a bad experience and didn't return. Then, suddenly, the "OPEN" light in the window dimmed with a cold finality. Exit *The Artisan Cafe* and *Jim's Little Store* and *Lois Elizabeth's Cafe*. Sad, sad, sad.

Food being food, however, local blacks (and a fair number of whites) do support their own version of a cafe in Mama's Restaurant, less a coffee shop or meat-and-three luncheonette than my little town's answer to fine dining. Here, under glowing chandeliers and football games on the TV screens, sitting on plastic chairs at tables with centerpieces of artificial camellias, you can open the fairly elaborate menu and choose rib-eye steaks and well-constructed salads served on gold metallic salvers, while appreciating the efforts at local style and finesse.

On an equally happy note, my little town has two excellent nursing homes to take care of its sick and old, mostly widows, recovering from hip replacements and bypasses and "the sugar" or dying from diabetes or "heart failure" or cancer. The competent staffs, both black and white, appear to have a more generous feel for racial justice than can be seen elsewhere in town; they treat the ill and old of both races with patience and grace. Perhaps because of the integration of the staff, the nursing homes, so crucial to the social life of the town, are almost always full; to reserve a bed sometimes takes "pull" of one sort or another. On Sundays after church, you have to get there early to find a parking space.

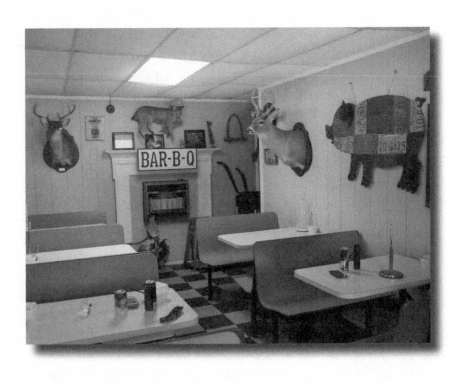

And so vestiges of life hang on, fragile but determined. Sadly, these vestiges of life are often closely aligned with death. Or, more accurately, decay. To measure the meaning of this seductive decay, the phenomenon Thomas Mann referred to as "the voluptuousness of doom," please excuse my indulgence in a medium known for a greater connotative power than mere prose:

The tall weeds bending beside the cracked asphalt.
The snake curled on the path beside the sagging porch.
The rusting car on blocks in the drive.
The lawn thick with unmown grass.

Where did these signposts come from? When did they know they were needed? When did emptiness begin on this block and not farther out, when did the silence of crickets scrape across the ear like needles, obliterating the echoes of voices raised in songs and anger?

Someone must have known. At one time, a man must have recognized the meaning of the darkened windows. At one time, a woman must have reflected on the paint scaling the walls of the abandoned gym.

The rutted street remembers (vaguely) when it first felt the tires of fewer and fewer cars, then only the paw-thumps of wild dogs scampering through the starless night.

Who is to blame?

Who can cry out for the neglected stones in the cemetery?

Who can protect the little library, its unread books inert on the untouched shelves?

Had enough? It's enough to drive you to drink.

Isolation

Some people like to travel to Australia because they say it reminds them of America in the 1950s. The subtext of that sentence seems to mean Australia is safe, predictable, does not need to be *made great again.*

But why travel so far? These erstwhile travelers would save thousands of dollars if they would instead visit Lovelady.

The wish to preserve, to avoid, to exclude, to live as though one were worlds away from the rest of the continental United States—just as Australia was worlds away from the rest of the world—is felt as strongly by the citizens of my little town as by those in Melbourne.

This feeling comes naturally, based on geography. My little town lies at the dead center of 724 square miles of barely incorporated land, with an average density of eight people per each of those square miles. It is an hour and a half to Birmingham. It is more than an hour to Tuscaloosa. It is an hour and a half to Montgomery. Between us and these cities lie miles of forests on both sides of the highways, or else long stretches of cotton and soybean fields, with houses interrupting the setting just enough to make you notice how rarely they appear. Hospitals are far enough away that stroke

victims are jeopardized. A decent restaurant is at least thirty minutes away. A decent supermarket is at least thirty minutes away. A decent haircut (for white men) is a half-hour away. Black men are more fortunate, in the sense that they can count on decent hair care at the local Sanitary Barbershop.

This remoteness, which necessarily imposes agrarian ways and values on the life of Lovelady, produces effects both common and uncommon: an appreciation of nature, a severe engagement with weather, a chance for men to leave the womenfolk behind by getting on a tractor or out in the woods. Surrounded by farms that need cultivation, and forests which beg for hunters, and streams that love fishermen, a society materializes that is unimaginable in any city. How can a person living mere blocks away from a Gristede's or a Publix or a Ralph's adequately appreciate the little produce stand selling fresh tomatoes and peaches which appears next to our Dollar General every July? Or the dangers of too much rain sitting in the field? How can one laugh at the camouflage-decked men's *Duck Dynasty*-styled beards in the hardware store, the hunting dogs hanging out of their trucks' passenger windows? Why should my white neighbors in the country not be proud of their disdain of "government," i.e., federal programs, when they can see so little benefit from them, unneedful as they are of public transport (they have their trucks) and smooth sidewalks (they don't walk much) and better crime prevention (they have their guns) and convenient airports (where would they be going in a plane)? Why should their politics not reflect this hands-off attitude? Of course, blacks, so dependent on a centuries-old patriarchy, share an opposing perspective, one which we will come to. Government grants and government programs are their life-blood.

This remoteness also allows some of us, many of us, to allow our memories to effect the distortion with which they are commonly credited. The empty distances alter the passage of time; the influences on so many American lives—the media, the stock market, fashion, Hollywood—hold little sway. Many of our white citizens remember the Eisenhower Years as America at its apex: the town was still growing, public schools were "quality controlled," the social position of the races was fixed, and Cuba was just another place to go on vacation.

These citizens can sit and tell you, as a past president of the Chamber of Commerce told me during a birthday lunch at Mama's Restaurant, that "I just wish things would go back [to] the way they were." This phrase, so replete with a privileged nostalgia, is the very quotation often uttered by supporters of a recent President, as they attempt to frame their fantasies of the past.

To a remarkable extent, my lunch companion need not have worried about going backwards in time. In our little town, we live in a world immaculate of modernity, or modernity as expressed in the culture of the last fifty years. No Beatles. No Streisand. No Dylan. No Lou Reed. No Pinter or Albee. No Abbie Hoffman. No *Village Voice*. No fond memories of Vietnam protests or Woodstock or waterbeds or pet rocks or leisure suits. No independent films. Few Jews. No international films. No radical chic or Lenny Bernstein or Tom Wolfe. No gay bars. No American Songbook. No international cuisines. No Philip Glass. No Balanchine. No Warhol. No Pop Art.

No blockbusters at the local theater. No "Free Nelson Mandela" t-shirts. No rock concerts. No—

You get the point. Time seems to have been suspended just past the fictional autumn when Harper Lee wanted us to believe Atticus Finch was setting things right in Maycomb. But we are not Maycomb. We are not Hooterville. We are not even Mayberry. We do not live in that sort of fictional vacuum. We do have a sense of history. Although an island in the middle of a lost cultural lake, my little town acknowledges all that has happened since Sputnik, since the Kennedy assassination, since The Day The Music Died. But acknowledging and assimilating are not quite the same, are they? Proud of our ability to exclude any unwanted influences, we live on unembarrassed, happy in our own ways and replete with pride in our discriminatory powers.

And in many cases the pride is understandable. To have deflected even a handful of the extreme shifts in popular culture during the last five decades is seen, in the minds of many in my little town, as an achievement. Due to their cemented sense of self, my neighbors have discerned that many of these shifts would not end happily for their particular tribe, one which perceives the post-1960s culture as having produced little beyond institutional mistrust, identity politics, fake wars, gender fluidity, ugly religious divisions, intergenerational strife, and, most notably, a loss of economic and political power. And, to agree with my white neighbors, much of contemporary popular culture *is* debased, derivative, devoid of competence, a frothy turbulence of one media-manufactured moment after another, all supported by a rabid commercialism.

So, in place of any current notion of popular culture, a locally created, more artistically traditional "culture" exists below the surface of my little town. This culture, determinedly white, prefers the classics of its race: Mozart over Moby, fiddles over amplifiers, Wordsworth over Williams. It is attuned to a time when technique mattered. Our culture is one in which people still play sonatas on the piano, vocalize for church solos, paint landscapes and portraiture rather than abstracts.

And they do so with a competitive level of talent; they might have "made it" had they had the ambition and vision to pursue goals more self-rewarding (and realized elsewhere). I have befriended colonels who can create on canvas the most beautiful cows, a librarian whose photos of empty farmhouses and barns will make you weep, a pianist with the passion of Lang Lang, and fiddlers who understand that the blues, if played with conviction, will leave you anything but sad. But this colonel, this pianist, these fiddle players, believed in others first, family first. True to the whites-only local Scouting tradition experienced by so of many of them, they believed in service before self. They believed in their little town. So they stayed. And they worked. And they raised families. And they went to church and took each day as it came, until their youthful ambitions were subsumed by mortgage payments and tap dance recitals, and before they knew it, grandchildren.

In the face of these new generations, some of them, some of us loyal to our decidedly white traditions, hang on to the old culture, the 1950s ways, ways that allow for little integration. Some of us still lament the poor hands we get at Tuesday's bridge club luncheon.

Some of us still worry about our solo in the Christmas cantata. Mothers still hope that their daughters will win first prize in the beauty pageant. Fathers still boast that their eight-year-old son shot a three-point buck. Memorial Day is still marked by fervent, tear-washed celebrations on the courthouse square, evermore flags flown evermore proudly, as growing numbers of local service men and women are remembered in ever-lengthening prayer lists.

Supporting this pride in the old ways, however, lies a staggering lack of imagination, most noticeably on a personal level. At least among us whites.

When, for lack of a more engaging conversational gambit, I once asked a student at the military institute where he would go on his dream vacation, he answered that he was fine where he was, thank you.

"I want to stay here the rest of life," he announced flatly. ("Here" was a farm near Benton, Alabama.) Further probes about his choice produced only circular logic. *Here I know. Here is best. What I know is best.*

Such is the degree of imagination among many of the natives, black and white. And such is the degree of incuriosity. Not once during the time I have lived in my little town have I been asked about my history, my life before I lived here. Rarely does anyone inquire about my family, or friends, or where I have gone on vacation. On the rare occasion that I am asked, no follow-up questions occur. The conversation dies, and I am left to consider exactly what discourse rules force me to express further interest in someone who obviously has so little interest in me.

What lies at the root of this incuriosity? At first, it seems a radical, and willful, alternative to the advice the author Joan Didion once quoted British journalist Jessica Mitford's governess as cautioning her to remember at all times: "You're the least important person in the room and don't forget it."

But people in my little town are not self-effacing, surprised, if anything, at anyone else's *lack* of interest in their lives. Nor are they particularly shy. No one should mistake their incuriosity for the discretion so often thought a part of Southern good manners. People in my little town can talk about their dogs' gastro-intestinal problems, their familial hiccups, their *own* hospital procedures, with an elastic sense of detail better reserved for an oncologist explaining to a patient the position of a tumor.

No, an intricate self-protection is at work, a wish to remain outside any influence that does not come from ourselves and our community and our religion and our customs. And this may be said of both races. If this intractability seems a predictable definition of tribalism, it is a tribalism intensified by scale, by an unmitigated in-breeding of values in a very small space and throughout many generations.

It is also a tribalism often expressed with a joyful nose-thumbing at political correctness, let alone civility toward other parts of the American quilt.

For instance: a friend—yes, a friend—at the military institute expressed outrage when I questioned the need to allow the monuments to the Confederate generals to remain standing in public spaces.

Her reaction was swift and fierce. "Those are *my* people, *my* ancestors!" she exclaimed. "They fought and *died* for their beliefs. Why would we not honor them? Look at all the streets named after Martin Luther King!"

But, I countered, Martin Luther King did not advocate war or violence or secession; he could be seen by many as a positive force.

"But *we* don't see him as positive," she continued. "Look at all the trouble he caused!"

Or, another example:

A writer for the local paper once complained to me about the realtors in my little town: "I don't know why they keep selling homes to people who should never be living here."

I asked him what particular sales he was referencing.

"Those Mexican and French people," he said without hesitation, specifying some recent arrivals who bought the old Campbell house. He then looked more directly at me. "And you."

He paused. "Just kidding," he added.

But he was not.

In just such isolation does ignorance breed. And ignorance breeds fear, and fear, suspicion—of outsiders, of Mexicans and French people. And when those outsiders arrive, as they inevitably do, a sour anger—born of jealousy, of helplessness, of regret—sweeps aside everything that came before it, leaving only the blunt realization that there may be no one left to be angry at except the face in the mirror.

The Economy

The economy of my little town? Dismal, a phantom.

No industry. No opportunity. No reason to stay. No reason to come back.

And, if you do stay, not much of a future. Remove the two colleges and where are the opportunities? There are few "careers" here. Why plan on a future? Why look to job training programs when there are so few jobs, except maybe an administrative support position in one of the colleges, or factory work at the Tek-Pak plant, the only factory in town, a white low-slung building that turns out plastic containers for room deodorizers and vaginal products?

What is the point of ambition when, as a young woman, the most you can hope for is a position in public education, or one in bookkeeping, or cleaning houses? What is the point of ambition when, as a young man, the most you can hope for is licensure as an accountant, an electrician, a plumber?

And, anyway, why bother with ambition when you have to move away to realize its benefits? And move away with what money? And move away from your family when your family is your *life*?

Which explains why the occasional explosion of a meth lab out in the country does not surprise anyone. You have to make money somehow. Which explains why farming still determines the dreams of so many local boys, why buying a truck and finding someone to marry and (temporarily) escaping the sterility of it all is such a pattern. Which explains the extravagantly hopeful expressions on the faces in the wedding photos in the Lifestyle section of the *Times-Standard*, the heightened intensity of the Experience of Marriage in the lives of so many local young women.

Their hopes often end up in tatters, however. Divorce is frequent in my little town, as is infidelity. Is it because of the dismal economy? Or because a "fling" becomes the next best thing to a vacation for many natives, namely those who cannot afford to get away?

The reality of the state of the local economy was once seen on what was called Trade Day, a large monthly outdoor rummage sale held in the parking lot of a shopping center that never quite took off. Trade Day was simply another name for bartering, a form of cashless negotiation that became popular during last century's Great Depression. Used to obtain food and various other services, this system acted in my little town as an informal kind of bank, a bank that came alive on certain Saturday mornings. Used tricycles, wedding dresses, romance novels, kitchen utensils, partial sets of china, and other throwaways of the poor were lined up in boxes around the parking lot for perusal. This system was built on trust; you needed to be able to depend on the person with whom you were trading, an arrangement which worked well in a town of fewer than three thousand people, among neighbors who could point out a haggler apt to pull off a bit of nefariousness.

Trade Day was always busiest just after the government checks appeared in the mailbox. My little town could not exist without its government checks: checks for that "bonus" child, checks for disability, checks for old age, checks for military service, checks of every kind, checks which keep the economy limping along. The first weekend of the month, the lines at the bank teller windows and the grocery store and the drug store speak to this fleeting wealth. A week later, the lines are gone, and we've relaxed back into our perpetual state of poverty.

Or perhaps, if you expand your range of vision, you see that the lines are not precisely gone; they have merely reappeared down Pickett Street at the Dollar General. Although my little town may scorn the thought of chain stores, it makes an exception for Dollar General, as do similarly struggling American towns and cities hosting the 16,278 others of its kind. Much as with Lovelady's nursing homes, the aisles of its Dollar General serve as common ground for both races; no matter the color of skin, the power of cheap paper towels seems to defeat any embarrassed admission that times are hard. Add to the addictive discounting the natives' almost inborn frugality and you can better comprehend how even Dollar General's harsh fluorescent lighting and sloppily overstuffed shelves did not deter the shoppers in my little town when the new store opened a few years ago. A new store, as long as it is a new Dollar General, is cause to celebrate in Lovelady. Walmart, eat your heart out!

Education

The quality of the educational system of my little town? As with the economy. Tragic, a phantom.

That my little town still conceives of itself as "The College City," its civic nickname, seems literally fantastic when you consider that the two colleges, here since the 1830s, are attended by almost none of the children who grew up in Huntley County or the Black Belt. Meanwhile, Lovelady Academy, the private (meaning "white") K–12 school, has trouble keeping its doors open, while the public (meaning "black") high school struggles with results of state test scores in the seventeen percent passing range for reading and in the fifteen percent proficiency level for math. Efforts to set up a charter school may succeed (and can be heard over the protests of the County Board of Education), but where will the millions of dollars in seed money come from?

What caused this disastrous, distressing educational "system"?

The least politically correct answer?

Integration.

Into the carefully segregated school system of my little town, integration introduced—not gradually, not with an eye toward the mind-bending challenge of mixing together races of colossally different backgrounds, not with any awareness of context—a sudden gush of students from homes where reading was often an anomaly, where abstract thought was mainly a religious concern, where an appreciation of the staples of mid twentieth-century public school education—Shakespeare and the French and Indian War and "higher" math and civics—had never really existed or existed from a contrary perspective. Forget the headlined victories of "opening up" public restaurants and bathrooms; in the classroom, integration attempted to achieve a more formidable triumph: choosing a public space so culturally rule-bound and freighted with a curriculum dependent on such segregated relevance that, for long into the future and unless transformed, it will corrode the quality of education to which one race is accustomed and ignore the disadvantages under which the other race suffers.

These words may seem harsh, almost incomprehensible coming from someone so steeped in the religion of equal opportunity, but I have lived among the results of integration in my little town and have realized how unintentionally harmful it has been, how many years my little town will require to fully realize its noble promise.

Any discussion about education in my little town convinces even the most casual observer that the determined segregation that still exists in the local educational system has produced a consequence that is tragically ironic and now seemingly irrevocable: the decades of lynching and Jim Crow and profiling has succeeded in creating the "ideal" result—not only a segregated class, but a segregated culture, one which no longer respects its "betters" or wants to be like them or, in this context, wants to know the same facts. What is the language of Shakespeare compared to that of Lil Nas X? Why would the study of American history begin not with Columbus but with the horses and troopers on the Edmund Pettus Bridge?

To further complicate matters of education, academic disciplines in Lovelady's curricula sometimes seem written from utterly contrary world views. The use of the plural "curricula" is intentional, especially in the case of American history. The public (black) school and the private (white) school employ wildly divergent sets of facts, and interpretations of those facts, about what occurred in the nineteenth and twentieth centuries in the South. Lovelady is not unique in this respect. Often, the interpretation in Southern (white) private schools reflects the underlying mistrust of the more diverse perspective of public education as practiced in the North. Think of the Texas State Board of Education and its partisan revisions of the state's social studies curriculum a few years ago and the attitude reveals itself clearly. Or consider the 1619 Project, for that matter. You soon stop asking questions about why so few parents in my little town, even those who can afford it, send their children North for college. In the North lie aberrant ideas, liberal professors, religious "tolerance," unholy suggestions, exposure to deviltry. In the North lies the abyss. An unspoken narrative suggests that children come back home from the North as altered beings—argumentative, suspicious of the old ways, angry at the status quo.

Nowhere is the accepted effect of a Northern education on a rural Southern adolescent captured more dramatically, or accurately, than in the short story "Revelation" by Flannery O'Connor, herself

familiar with both a small Southern town and a Northern education.

A quick summary: As Ruby Turpin, the prideful protagonist of that story, waits in a doctor's office for her appointment, O'Connor uses a combination of interior monologue and conversation to reflect Ruby's self-serving opinions of the other patients. Among these souls waiting to see the doctor is Mary Grace, a girl who has gone North to college but who has been sent home due to what seems to be a mental breakdown. ("She goes to Wellesley College," says her mother, sitting beside her. "In Massachusetts ... [she's] a girl who never smiles. Just criticizes and complains all day long.")

And, even worse, *reads* all day long, books being another poisonous influence of the North and the odious World. Although Ruby is able to place each of the other people in the waiting room on a precise rung on her local social ladder, Mary Grace remains a mystery to her, all the more so because the girl concentrates an ugly, hate-filled stare at Ruby, sensing behind her hard-wrought gentility and sticky politeness a hideous smugness.

So enraged does Mary Grace become at Ruby's conversation with the other patients that she finally attacks her, throwing the book she has been reading at her and hitting her in the face, while wishing her to "go back to hell where you came from, you old wart hog." O'Connor allows her troubled, injured protagonist an exit home from the waiting room and then drops her into a narrative climax which wrenches her entire social order free from its moorings.

At the end of the story, Ruby is out in the barnyard feeding her pigs under a threatening sky. Looking up at the heavens, still confused and fearful by what she experienced in the doctor's office, she has a hallucinatory vision, in which a horde of her neighbors ascends to heaven, but in a dangerously *wrong* social order, with unchurched blacks and white trash ahead of the faithful, among whom Ruby sees herself. As a final protest, she opens her mouth to shout out her objection to the skies but is unable to utter a sound.

Ruby is at an impasse, as is my little town's educational system—riven by opposing cultures, and classes, and political persuasions, and even faiths. These impasses underline why you will find few white teachers in the black schools in Huntley County. The few are usually young men and women sent from the federal Teach for America program, novices imported to provide hope, a font of inspiration, to an education system that is withering from within. These young men and women come every year, hungry to make a change. They teach for a while, and then leave, often with newly hardened hearts, sclerotic from the same bitterness about their experience with public education as that of Lovelady's natives.

As they depart, they leave behind an educational system at war with itself, divided by race, searching for a common relevance, and made helpless by well-meaning federal mandates. You end up wondering if all the magnificent intentions of *Brown vs. Board of Education* were in the best interest of any of the parties involved.

Chicken Salad

My fork is poised to descend into a greedy portion of Betty Lou's chicken salad. The mild colors of the shredded chicken and Miracle Whip and the bits of celery and green onion (*tiny* bits, please!) signal their readiness to be devoured. My fork drops down, dipping into the soft textures and coming up with a decent amount ("decent" meaning it can be put on a Ritz cracker) and directing itself upward and forward, as if on its own power. A mouthful falls onto my tongue. I wait for a moment before biting down, enjoying the smell of the chicken salad, a tangy, pickle-y odor mixed with a whiff of poultry. As I begin chewing, the textures rub against my tongue, the smoothness of the mayonnaise barely concealing the roughness of the shredded chicken.

Can one ever be this satisfied?

I should not even try to put into words the significance of chicken salad to the diet and sense of well-being of my little town. If it were only possible, I would instead paste a spoonful onto the pages of this book and allow you to taste what my little town cannot survive without, cannot escape worshipping in beautiful china dishes at lunches, brunches, receptions, bridge club parties, church socials, pot lucks, all with the same surety once seen in Chris Evert's backhand.

Its consistent appearance at local events has little to do with recipe consistency. Nor is much attention paid to the original recipe, scuttled in much the same Southern manner as with the traditional recipe for pimento cheese spread, another of its classics. Certainly, the hostesses of my little town do not concern themselves with anything like the chicken salad first served by Town Meats in 1863 in Rhode Island—a mix of leftover chicken with mayonnaise, tarragon, and grapes. (A newcomer to Lovelady once invented what he called "Rooster Salad," using tarragon. It never caught on.)

Although the hostesses go every which way with their recipe of this classic, their loyalty to their own version borders on the obsessive. The (always polite) sparring over ingredients, the intensity of the divergent passions about the appropriateness of grapes or apple slices, the strong opinions about sweet relish versus dill relish, the unswerving allegiance to Miracle Whip, the (to some) heretical idea of Duke's mayonnaise—these issues swirl together to create a whipsaw of discussion that touches on differences of class and education. This point follows two rough rules of thumb: the poorer the cook financially, the less likely the use of Hellman's. The more "country" the cook, the more likely the taste of sweet pickle relish.

Chicken salad is only the proverbial foot-in-the-door to my little town's embrace of food. In all its glory, food rules. Food is love. Food glues people together to a degree even a church revival cannot touch. The postmortem casseroles, the fundraising barbecue dinners, the library chili cook-offs, the Valentine's Day bake sales dominate the civic calendar as testimonies to this truth. Interestingly, much of the food at these events seems frozen in the tastes and recipes of the 1950s: deviled eggs, sweet puddings, cheese balls, chicken cas-seroles of all kinds. Congealed salads. Bourbon balls at Christmas. A preponderance of pies, pound cakes, brownies.

The texture of all these dishes shares another quality: a softness, an un-chewy quality quite apart from—sometimes in defiance of—the natural state of the plant or animal being served. A stubborn resistance to the modern demands of healthful eating that entered the larger culture in the 1980s fits neatly into this 1950s preference for boiling, for steaming, for blanching, for frying the hell out of—or into—many foods. Green beans melt in your mouth. Carrots are cooked to a slippery smoothness. More often than not, a coating of grated cheese—on salads, on chili, on potatoes—blurs other tastes, swallows them in a kind of edible plastic wrap.

Sugar is not optional in this land of sweet tea and fig cakes and divinity candy and Little Debbies. The seemingly mandatory affection for sugar in my little town is only slightly tempered by the awareness of its viperous charms, not the least of which is the lethal pleasure of eating it even as inches appear on waistlines, rolls of fat bloom under the arms, layers mounting on the back, chin upon chin upon chin.

Because of this push-pull between the love of the sugared and a simultaneous vanity about their figures, many of the women in my little town approach a meal with amusing illogic. I once heard a hairdresser order a lunch delivery during my haircut. "Two corn dogs," she said into her cell, "and a Diet Coke." She flipped her phone closed and looked at me in the mirror. "I just *have* to watch my weight," she vowed piously. I waited in vain for a giggle.

But might I also add that the people in my little town enjoy food to a degree and in a variety of ways that shame the careful forkfuls and starved necklines of their counterparts sitting over a salad in Manhattan or San Francisco. They understand the array of powers food has at its disposal, how many occasions can employ food as focus, food as rationale, food as the ultimate link to being human: sickness, recoveries from operations, weddings, pilgrimages, new babies (when a stork "flag" is stuck in the front lawn).

Even in death, food serves as the supreme earthly balm. The food—the staggering amount of food—served at some of these visitations would never be found up North. Here, in my little town, food replaces whiskey at the wake: Seven Layer Salad, Fire 'n Ice Salad, deviled eggs, pimento cheese finger sandwiches, chicken salad finger sandwiches, pasta salad drenched in "ranch" dressing, chicken casseroles, tomato aspic, cheese balls, chicken noodle casserole, broccoli salad, baked ham, fried chicken, "funeral" potatoes, "truck stop" potatoes, macaroni and cheese, ambrosia, brownies, banana pudding, caramel cake, lemon ice box cake, pound cake, banana bread—people get "drunk" on food, eat to soothe their misery.

Perhaps you can now understand why the degree of obesity in my little town is forgivable.

And then there are the church meals, especially the soup lunches, which provoke not only the sweetest of impulses among those hunkered over the cornbread and pecan pie, but also a rare brand of ugliness that can quickly call into question the very sanity of those women standing by the huge pots in the kitchens of the Fellowship Halls. To wit: the poisoned soup . . .

Poisoned Soup

I tell The Tale of the Poisoned Soup at my peril. Lovelady is a little town, and discretion can be easily manipulated, confidences quickly lost. However, in the interest of accurate portrayals, and with the allowance for some changes of name, I will tell a story which I hope will be instructive. And funny.

The morning in question dawned at seventy-eight degrees. The air, a torpid marinade of heat and humidity, had by noon turned the late fall day of The Soup Luncheon into a sweaty hunt for air-conditioned space. Inside the kitchen of the little church, the two lead players in this piece, Miss Shirley and Mrs. Christine, both relatively new to the parish, were eager to establish that solid reputation a cleverness with food preparation can quickly confer in my little town.

(At this point you might notice we have ascended into the ethereal literary world of Barbara Pym, the novelist of English village social life. Miss Pym could spend hundreds of pleasurable pages tracking the terribly refined dominion of the combative icons known as church ladies, those women wrestling obsessively with tribulations such as longings for the rector, luncheon place settings, liturgical anomalies, and the niceties of congregational rank.)

She would understand why The Soup Luncheon has remained a constant on the calendar of my little town since the Devil was a baby, or for at least the last twenty years. She would also be pleased with its sense of ritual. For example, in obeisance to some unwritten, but seminal, custom, the church ladies required the soup be prepared by the newer members of the parish.

One of those newcomers was Miss Shirley Hudgens. Miss Shirley had appeared out of nowhere, as do so many newcomers to my little town, trailed by rumors of jobs in Iraq, previous husbands, remote children, and unsettled behaviors which had pushed her from location to location. After her arrival, she bought a small house and joined the church. She was pretty, not in the usual sorority-girl, matte-foundation manner that many women in my little town preserve into perpetuity, but rather in the wide-calved, hearty style of a drum majorette; a broad smile and a full figure added to her uncommonly flirtatious way with the local men. At the same time, she made every effort to engage the local women, although her coquettish air, tall stature, and inevitable pony tail separated her in matters of taste and style from many.

Despite her unconventional appearance and occasional social gaffe, however, the church ladies offered Miss Shirley the chance to participate in preparing the soup, made from a recipe the ancestry of which had remained unchanged for decades. Not that it had been unilaterally well-received over the years. Murmurs of "tastelessness," stories about the "surprisingly boring" mix of ingredients, haunted the yearly reviews.

Provoking these comments was the fact that the actual recipe has remained a secret as inviolate as a Masonic rite. As a result, what follows is unverified and based only on many tastings:

THE RECIPE (makes eight servings)

1 lb. lean ground beef
1 small onion, diced
Salt and pepper to taste
2 cans of mixed vegetables, undrained
1 can petite diced tomatoes, undrained
1 can water
1 large potato, cubed and peeled
5 beef bouillon cubes
½ teaspoon Italian seasoning

The rules for making individuals' batches of The Recipe were as unswerving as they were clear: All cooks must use the same proportions and ingredients. Each must make at least twenty servings. And all must have brought their prepared soup to the Fellowship Hall by mid-morning of the lunch.

Despite an animated exchange between two ladies about the table placement of the salt and pepper shakers, preparations in Fellowship Hall went smoothly, and the luncheon began at 11 a.m. People packed around the long, plastic-topped tables, eager to enjoy their portion of soup, cornbread, and a sweet. However, as the story goes, things began to go awry when a commotion was heard at Table

#3. Pete, a man not known for complaining, took one spoonful of his soup and suddenly spat it out in a napkin.

"It's spoiled," he gagged, pointing to his soup. "Or *something.*"

"*Here,*" said a lady beside him, as she put her spoon in his bowl. After a sample, she put her napkin to her mouth. "Oh, dear!" she said. "It's *definitely* gone off."

She jumped out of her seat and gestured to a friend to meet in the kitchen, where a group of women had gathered around a pot of soup warming on the stove. Shirley, helping serve a dessert at another table, sensed something was afoot and followed the exodus to the kitchen.

Upon entering the room, she looked the women over slowly, one by one. "What's the problem?" she asked, gesturing toward the pot in question. "That's *my* soup."

The women looked away from her in unison. After an awkward silence, one of the bolder among them remarked carefully that the soup "might have turned."

"That's impossible," Shirley replied, puzzled. "I made it yesterday." She grabbed a spoon, dipped it into the pot, tasted a mouthful, paused, and then looked up in shock. Seconds passed, difficult seconds, seconds during which reputations in the little church are shattered and enmities entrenched. Finally, she found the words, speaking in a fierce whisper.

"It didn't taste like this when I brought it in this morning," she began, looking from face to face, all frozen in horror. Her face reddened as her eyes began to widen. "I know *exactly* what happened." She paused, adding dramatic effect to the moment:

"*One of you poisoned my soup.*" Her voice took on a nasty edge as she contemplated the betrayal. "Who did it? Which one of you poisoned my soup?"

The church ladies were stunned into silence until Mary Margaret Reed responded, "Shirley, no one poisoned your soup. Maybe it spoiled last night. Did you leave it sitting out?"

Her mouth dropped open. "What do you think I am?" she shouted. "I would never leave soup just sitting out." Then, gripped by a sudden thought, she glared at Melanie Curtis. "*I know you did it. I know you don't like me. I've seen the way you look at me.*"

Melanie, never one to back down from an accusation, began to defend herself. The argument quickly achieved the volume of a locker room after a women's field hockey game. Guests in the dining hall put down their spoons and listened intently as shrill Southern vowels piled atop each other, reminding everyone that few sounds can be as ugly as that of rural Alabama women at variance.

Suddenly, in a final gesture, Miss Shirley snapped her fingers in Mrs. Melanie's face, whirled around, and headed out of the church, spine stiff with righteousness. She is now rarely seen outside her house except for late-night trips to Food Value.

And so ends The Tale of the Poisoned Soup. Interestingly, there has been minimal ecclesiastical outreach to her after this incident. As such, the tale has fallen off the scale of titillation from church outrage to an amusing story appropriate for lagging conversations at birthday parties. Nothing about it is now too scandalous or too liturgically rarified to disqualify it from repetition, except, that is, the irksome thought that this kind of moment is exactly that which raises doubts about spiritual commitment, spiritual priorities among members of the little church. Is it that a small church ambience magnifies the silliness of this sort of dispute? Is it the result of a peculiar sort of religious fervor? Or is it simply church women waging some sort of atavistic war, struggling to cement positions and create alliances?

Family

Much is made of "family" in my little town, and, frankly, much should be. "Family" as a concept, built on generational outreach, and "family" as a reality, staunchly nuclear and stripped of quotation marks, live on here, irrespective of that politicized sense of "family" values. Here, family has more to do with history, less with politics. Fathers put time and attention toward their sons' maturity, nurture the local strictures defining the nature of manhood. They hunt together, they watch football together, they *play* football together for as long as knees allow, fathers coaching sons to throw a perfect pass or fake an opponent out of position. Mothers still teach their daughters how to sew, or bake a pound cake, or arrange a centerpiece. Motherhood is still sacred. Pregnancies are welcomed with the same fervor Ruth Gordon welcomed Mia Farrow's child in *Rosemary's Baby*. "Sir" and "ma'am" are still honorifics used respectfully by younger family members.

Through these customs, generations flow sweetly into each other; continuity is maintained. Memories are literally created from specific bits of the present. Comment on the wonders of a blueberry cobbler to a hostess and she'll smile, thank you, and comment,

"That was Grandmother Blixton's recipe." Although you never met her (she may have been dead for years), Grandmother Blixton suddenly comes alive, the hostess drops years in age, and the image emerges of the two women in a long-ago kitchen, grandmother and granddaughter laughing and teaching and learning together, bathed in the tender light of what Norman Rockwell might have illustrated as "Love."

How easily one can sentimentalize this current of affection that runs so deeply through many of the families in my little town! I am certainly guilty of adding my own layer of nostalgia to the many pictures of family life I have witnessed in my years here. How, indeed, can one avoid the urge to idealize the following story told by an elderly friend who lives down the street?

"Oh, I remember many evenings," she began, a smile taking over her face, "when my mother would sit down at the piano, my father would grab his tuba and my brother his saxophone, and they'd play some of those lovely old songs together: 'On the Sunny Side of the Street' and 'You Are My Sunshine' and 'Alexander's Ragtime Ball.' We had a long porch across the front of the house, and, with the music coming through the open windows, I'd put on my tap shoes and dance from one end of the porch and back, pretending that the front lawn was full of people, ready to applaud."

But, as in all families, a little rain must fall. The sweetness of this image is complicated by knowing that the speaker's mother had a gift for cruelty, that her older brother died of alcoholism, that the family carried a genetic defect, impervious to advanced diagnosis or warning. None of these facts could ignore a more salient truth:

during these tribulations, the family stayed together, continued to celebrate each other at significant birthdays, at graduations, at christenings. As a result, my friend is now beloved by four children, twelve grandchildren, and eight great-grandchildren, all of whom plan to care for her as she grows older.

With this kind of example, is it any wonder that the men and women of my little town are proud of their ancestry, hold on to each other less out of duty than love? They need no website or television program to help them track their roots. They simply go to their family Bible and refer to the family tree, to which generation after generation have added their names in beautiful calligraphy.

Apropos of this degree of familial history, I have another neighbor who, when asked how far back he could trace his roots, needed no time to respond. "Unfortunately, I can only go back to 1445, to my distant relative James of Thimtoft Manor in Yorkshire," he responded with a bit of rue in his voice. "But after that, it's clear sailing—right up the present generation."

Funerals

Death becomes my little town.

Its citizens are practiced at death; its population is dying faster than a chicken casserole disappearing at a field-hand lunch. The town's experienced response to death displays its talent for dignified protocol, its empathy and regard for neighbors, even newcomers.

These strengths remain singular, distinctive. Although Southern funerals have long been *sui generis* when compared to those of Vermont or Nebraska, the "Americanization" of the region (and the increasingly secular approach to the customs of death), has muted their peculiarity in many sections of the South.

Not so in my little town. Its funerals continue untouched by change. News of the end of a life still speeds through the streets, spurred less by a passion for gossip than by a closeness to the bereaved, for in my little town the "bereaved" is often a dear friend, the person you chat with in the grocery store aisle, the elderly lady whose yard you rake, the matron who always brings banana pudding to the church supper. Here, *people you know* die regularly, and so your reaction to this death is immediate.

At the same time, death in my little town is also universal, with an encompassing significance, because each death visibly shrinks our civic life, in the same alarming manner that assets in a portfolio shrink, that a mole darkens suspiciously. Our town's institutions and organizations collapse as deaths occur; putting on annual events becomes more desperate, then irrevocably harmed. *Now we have one less partner for the bridge foursome. Where will we find someone to play the organ on Sunday? There will never be another caramel cake like hers. We can't even keep the Chamber of Commerce going!*

So the intense sadness that accompanies death is layered with civic *and* personal implications which ripple through the landlines with an unsettling rhythm, creating a wave of literal death duties for the citizens. These duties are assigned, predictably, to the citizens who regularly perform them.

Marge will be responsible for the beverages at the visitation.

Edith has coordinated the casseroles.

Jim has organized the pallbearers.

Dan will be giving the eulogy.

As expected. As last week.

Added to this individual involvement in the process of death is the pride the local churches in my little town take in the professional quality of their funerals. These rites flow gracefully, often beautifully, buoyed by a production value worthy of a David O. Selznick film. A significant enhancement to these productions are the flower arrangements. Imagined by either of the two local florists or a lady renowned for her sense of composition and balance, these arrangements signify not only an enviable entry into the supernatural but also often telegraph the degree of respect for

the person in the coffin. I have seen arrangements worthy of a head of state, lilies and camellias and azaleas—all the gorgeous flowers available for a spring funeral in the Deep South—emerging as a glorious salute from a huge funeral urn.

And the touching expressions of familial love at these funerals! I do not recall seeing in the North—not at funerals in New England, not in the Midwest—a family arrayed in a half-moon around an open casket at a "viewing," smiling into the lens of a camera for a scrapbook photo, but I saw one in my little town. I also heard at another viewing an a capella shape-singing quartet, composed of four brothers of the deceased, each weeping as they rendered "In the Garden." I have seen a coffin careening down a summertime country road, pulled by a sweating boy on a bicycle. I have even conversed, in a graveside chat, with a man who was planning to reload his favorite shotgun with buckshot molded from a dead relative's cremated remains. Presumably, as a tribute to the deceased's passion for firearms, the shot would later be released in a treasured spot of the loved one, emerging from the muzzle in a puff of holy smoke.

In fact, living in such a close community has allowed me to embrace its funerals to a degree far more intimately than when I lived anonymously in large cities. I have been literally engaged by the funerals of my little town. I have hoisted to my shoulder caskets at military funerals and remained motionless during the ten-gun salute at the graveside. I have staggered to load the heavy coffins of friends into the back door of a 1992 Cadillac hearse. I have been moved by funerals of local celebrities, such as that of Mary Ward Brown, a superior writer of short stories, when the little

Episcopal Church was so crowded that the many people there to honor her were forced out of the sanctuary and had to wait in the adjoining Fellowship Hall to pay their respects to the family during the "visitation." I have attended funerals of black friends, in black churches, when I was the only pale face in the crowd, admiring the hats and flowers, listening to testimony after testimony about the bereaved, and verse after verse of passionate singing, all amplified to a thunderous degree.

Despite the deep divisions in my little town, and some predictable stylistic distinctions, funerals permit a contradictory, reassuring truth: death is blind to color. Its "sting" recedes when confronted with the shared tears and hugs at the back of the sanctuary, the casseroles left quietly at the back door, the sympathy cards, the prayer lists and heartfelt mentions across all sorts of worship services. As a result, the outreach of death accomplishes what so much of life in my little town cannot: it includes our citizens in exactly the kind of communion most needed for healing.

Religion

"Flip flops are the glass slippers
of the Jesus-loving."

—Seen on the T-shirt of a girl pumping gas

I fidget in the pew. I dream of future vacations, Oman, Sri Lanka. I take principled stances about controversial issues that will remain unuttered. I try to remember the verses of favorite Rogers and Hart tunes. I read random psalms in the back of the *Book of Common Prayer*. If at all, I pay only fractured attention to the service, concentrating on the melodies in the hymns and what a few of the women are wearing.

And I wonder, constantly, what these people are doing and thinking beside and around me. Why are they attending church? What does it mean to them? Does their attention wander? Do they feel especially devout reciting the Nicene Creed? Do they feel "born again" after a service? Do they attend because they want their children to grow up with the "right values"? Do they come for the flower arrangements? The "message" in the homily? Why are they so worshipful? Exactly what are they adoring?

These questions reveal my fatal detachment from the religious attitudes held by many of the citizens of my little town. The cord connecting their religion and their lives is so strong, so much of a given in so many activities, that some would be tempted to think of the degree of connection as "cultish." But that would be inaccurate. (After a few bourbons, you hear a great deal of irreverence about certain ministers and certain forms of worship.) More precisely, our churches are institutions, with all the earth-bound and regulatory issues inherent in that definition. And our citizens are indubitably institutionalists.

Without churches, my little town would not exist. Their institutional nature is uncontested enough that people in my little town still speak of the "unchurched," a word foreign to many outside the Deep South. (The term means, simply, that the person is nor a formally confirmed member of a congregation.) "I am saddened to hear that X was 'unchurched,'" said a pillar of one of the local congregations at a funeral. "I'll always think of him as 'lost.'"

I could not help but think of myself when I heard this comment. For decades, I rarely found myself inside a church, except to admire the architecture. In the places I lived, religion wasn't thought of as engaging enough to merit discussion.

Not that I lacked exposure to religion. I experienced a rainbow of doctrines in my youth. My parents, inveterate seekers of The Truth, "shopped" throughout their lives for a faith to which they could commit. I began my religious life as an Episcopalian, in a beautiful suburban cathedral in Bethesda, Maryland, where, as a three-year-old lost in the twilight of a magisterial nave, I was haunted by the melody of "Now the Day Is Over." We then moved to the country and became members of a tiny Church of God, where I stood in front of the congregation of farmers and sang "Jesus Wants Me for a Sunbeam" as a distant cousin pounded out the melody on a poorly tuned upright piano.

Then came the Baptists, the faith of my maternal grandparents. There, in the pink-gelled glow of a sanctuary modeled on a Greek amphitheater, I wore a mint-green polyester suit guaranteed to survive immersion in a fiberglass Baptismal font. The sacred moment was overseen by a pastor who, complete with an oily curl dangling over his forehead, resembled Burt Lancaster in the movie version of Sinclair Lewis's *Elmer Gantry*. Three years later, my family joined the First Presbyterian Church in a neighboring town. There, I was confirmed in a starchy ceremony characterized by stiff spines and strict finger-wagging about the Elect.

Finally, and somewhat futilely, we returned to the Mother Faith, back to a little Episcopal church that had once been a home of a small-scale industrialist, with a *porte cochere* and a velvety lawn thick with maple trees. My only memories of these services were my close examinations of the initials carved by bored children into the backs of the pews and the cake donuts that I would devour in a little room behind the kitchen during the "coffee hour."

Would I say that I was preternaturally irreverent, too aware of cant and posturing? I'm sure so. But why do I struggle with the idea of faith even now, to the degree that I often come home from church in my little town with a headache, sickened by my inclination to dismiss, to ridicule, to push away people and ideas meant only in kindness? When did this terrible urge to pick at doctrinal scabs begin?

A personal anecdote might answer some of these questions.

I am sixteen, sitting in the foolishly large living room of a home my parents cannot afford. Outside, snow is showering the bare branches of the trees, flakes blown by a terrible wind that sends drafts around the edges of the picture window. I have come home early from watching a high school basketball game because I had been shoved off the edge of a bleacher to make room for a boy more socially acceptable than I was.

After the shove, I landed with humiliating awkwardness on the cement floor of the aisle, parents and students struggling to get around me as I stood up. I looked briefly at the row of schoolmates, all laughing yet also slightly ashamed, their faces turned away at an angle so they could still witness my humiliation while hiding any visible embarrassment at their actions.

This incident should not have been terribly surprising, predicated as it was on my willful disrespect of one of the seminal tenets of the unwritten code of behavior common to American high schools everywhere: socially successful males must be members of a varsity sports team. That I had been on the varsity basketball team my first year of high school, that I had been president of the freshman class, that I had been the earnest squire of one of the most eligible girls were facts quickly and irrevocably rendered moot by a decision I made as I entered my sophomore year: no more team sports for me.

The dramatic results of this decision—the subsequent loss of the class presidency, the withdrawal of the girl's affections, the sudden shunning by friends who, weeks earlier, had been calling and calling to go to a movie—taught me less about the price paid for bucking conformity than about the more easily hidden costs of self-delusion. For my classmates were correct about me; they knew my game before I did, understood that I was neither inclined nor sincerely committed to squaring myself with what they needed me to be.

As I left the gymnasium, rushing out into the snowstorm, I somehow knew that everything had changed; what little "youth" I could still access had been lost when I hit the cement of the aisle floor. From that moment on, I would not be part of the passing parade, but the scout of a distant army, scanning the horizon for peril, visible and anticipated.

Walking down that lonely street, I could already see a threatening vision emerging through the falling snow. Familiar worlds tangled with worlds far less predictable, worlds with languages I would need to learn. Imaginary cities flared up out of nowhere. Impregnable-seeming clouds suddenly obscured otherwise clear views; strange faces floated in and out of the clouds, mixed with those of my parents, whom I saw crying and waving from a great distance.

Was this moment what they called an "epiphany," or a case of adolescent hormones, or merely a passing, albeit terribly vivid, incident common to teenagers everywhere? I have yet to answer this question, but I can say that this vision came so forcefully that I had to sit down in the middle of the sidewalk and shake myself.

Everything was suddenly foreign to me, to anything I knew, any system, any values, any culture, any set of experiences. "Right" and "wrong" suddenly needed a reappraisal. What was "right" for me would now, from this moment forward, be less clear. I was not just going down a road not taken. I was going off the road entirely, into a woods where what I learned in church or at school or through any familiar voice did not apply. I became in that instant a man of the world, and to a man of the world, the universe is a suburb. Nothing daunts, nothing frightens, anything goes.

When I arrived home and slammed shut the front door of my parents' home, I was sure of what I would say to them. I sat down by the fireplace and explained what had happened in the gym, what it meant to me and my future, what they could expect and not expect from that point on. I do not remember much of what they said, except my father's rather trenchant remark that I was going to find life more difficult, but possibly more rewarding.

Also, I added, I would not be attending church with them in the future. (Remember: I was sixteen.) I explained that for some time I had been merely occupying a pew, able to find no connection between my life and the Prayer of Humble Access. I did not feel like a "sinner," as imperfect as I knew I was. I could no longer recite the Nicene Creed with any conviction, nor could I imagine that most of my fellow parishioners understood it, either.

Entranced by this naively adamant perspective, I plowed on with my comments. My parents listened politely as I told them that faith in a Higher Power was quite enough for me. Youth Groups, Singspirations, Sunday Schools, sententious sermons, Bible verses steadfastly memorized to win pins and medals, all the events guaranteed to produce children of sound moral values, sickened me, riled me to a degree that I could no longer participate in what seemed preposterously out of touch with the life I knew I would be leading.

I delivered all this information in a passionate tirade. (I cannot recall standing up during the diatribe, but I can almost guarantee that the speech was accompanied by theatrical gestures.) After I had finished, my father put his Scotch down.

"Tell me," he said, smiling gently while unconsciously paraphrasing a comment the sociologist Daniel Bell remembers his rabbi telling him in a similar circumstance. "Do you think God will care?"

Suddenly feeling vulnerable, I left the room and within a year, my home and my parents, off to my new life. True to my word and that adolescent vision, for decade after decade, city after city, I treated Sunday morning not as a time for worship, but as a time to "catch up on things," do errands, make phone calls, sleep off a previous night's party.

So what was I doing here, now, so many years later, in my little town, again surrounded by ritualized piety and social lives constructed around "organized" religion? Trying to make a mockery of Thomas Wolfe? Or giving myself a second chance to take another look at the whole shebang? I was older now. I could be more "mature," more needful of things that others seemed to need, accept the things I couldn't change. Couldn't I?

I am here to tell you that I am making a valiant effort. I am a member of the vestry. I play the organ when the need arises. I have, against my better judgment, been recruited for the Altar Guild, which includes setting up the Lord's Table and arranging flowers for the reredos. The rector's patience with my repeated errors in achieving perfection in re-creating the order of the pyramid of sacred vessels, his wife's acceptance of my ability to turn a stunning assortment of flowers into something imagined by a chimpanzee, is exceeded only by their expressions of beatitude as they listen to me maul the Sanctus, my fingers clumsy with nerves.

The congregation is equally well-mannered about my difficulties and seems to express only the warmest sort of pity at my failings. Reactions encompass all the best effects that institutionalized religion showers on my little town: compassion, awareness of human frailty, generosity of spirit, respect for the elderly. These attributes are often given other names, such as "obedience" and "reverence" and "blessed assurance."

"Perfect submission, perfect delight" goes the song they sing so often. *"Visions of rapture now burst on my sight."*

The Bible, for many in my little town, is the wellspring of these raptures, and all this blessed assurance. The power of the Bible here—what happens in the name of the Bible—would give great joy to medieval priests. When, recently, I asked a librarian who is also a pillar of the Methodist Church how she liked her new pastor, she quickly replied, "Wonderful! He's Bible-based!"

The Bible and its words, preferably as they appear in the King James Version, are drummed into, memorized by, infused within, explained to the littlest ears of my little town, at an age when questioning the validity of these words is impossible, when the words mean nothing beyond strange groups of sounds and rhythms, repeated until they have an incantatory power.

And how could it be otherwise? Where, after all, was I living? Why did I not anticipate how tightly the Bible Belt would be cinched in the land of Southern Baptists? The Bible is the Word of God. The Bible is the Rock, the basis of all life, all thought. The Bible is inerrant and infallible, as stated in the 1978 *Chicago Statement on Biblical Inerrancy.*

And don't think for one minute that a word of it is metaphorical. Heaven is real. Hell is real. Eternal life is real. (You won't hear the phrase, "You only live once" very often in my little town.)

That this approach to biblical text was called into serious question sometime around the Scopes trial and continues to be called into question by many articulate, faithful Christians seems to carry little currency among almost all of the men and women faithfully going up the steps of the churches on Sunday morning in my little town.

You might even say these citizens are *indoctrinated* in their beliefs, their training beginning as it does at such an early age. And yet, despite the harsh connotations of the word, many worse types of control could be imposed.

One benefit common to all indoctrination is that it allows for certitude, a frame of mind increasingly rare outside my little town. In turn, this certitude of faith spills over into other, complementary, certitudes: of one's future, of social customs (bread-and-butter notes are still encouraged, for example), of Prelapsarian political preferences (the "lapse" occurring somewhere around 1964) and, ultimately, certitude about the world outside that of my little town.

Inversely, to harbor doubts about the Bible, let alone express them, is to drop into a terrifying void, to enter a twilight engineered by an incalculably evil enemy, one with an agenda of same-sex marriage, "socialized" medicine, "big" government, secular humanism, *Democrats*. Moreover, because Fox News is aired so frequently on so many televisions in the kitchens and dens of their houses (and in the waiting rooms of the doctors' offices and service centers of car dealerships), my friends sometimes have little ability to even acknowledge or frame their doubts, spiritual or otherwise. Diversity of opinions or perspectives are gutted *a priori*, leaving many citizens of my little town unreachable by logic, by fact, by science, by persuasion.

You don't mess with The Truth.

Should, by some unfortunate circumstance, any doubts about a religious or political opinion creep into one's consciousness and grant a victory to the other side—the Devil's side—in an election, in an argument with one's teenaged children, in a classroom—the situation quickly becomes desperate. The Apocalypse awaits. Armageddon is on the way. The world as we know it explodes, evaporating personal and social power. And as "our" power recedes and "we" slip down the social ladder and everything "we" know and understand is swept away from "us," the end time has arrived. (We are now firmly within the political purposes of St. Paul.) Which underscores the urgency behind the need for total agreement, the relative fury at independent thought, and, ultimately, the fear of compromise and peaceful solutions.

As is missing church. To miss even a Sunday or two of services is to invite questions. These questions are often delivered with an impish self-mockery, as though the questioner understands that this type of curiosity might be unwelcome or out-of-style. But they are delivered nonetheless. And to not answer them, or to deflect them, or even more dramatically, to imply that they are inappropriate, is to provoke an embarrassing backtracking in the questioner.

Church as habit, every Sunday and, depending on the denomination, every Wednesday evening. A habitual "blessing" spoken at meals, at civic functions, at political gatherings. Prayer as routine. Faith as routine. Acceptance of one's "lot" as routine. Acceptance, unquestioning acceptance, as the rule: acceptance of one's sinful soul, acceptance of your mother's cornbread recipe, acceptance of the inevitability of marriage and children, acceptance of commitment to friends and family, acceptance of death, acceptance of Heaven, acceptance of Hell.

Makes things simpler, doesn't it? Not much need for analysis. (Analysis just gets you into trouble, after all.) The unexamined life and unexplored faith are, in my little town, very worth living and very easy to live. They are enjoyed by many of my neighbors, many in my church "family." I am thinking now of the "book club" through which a well-meaning soul at my church attempted to encourage among the congregants an interest in exploring new approaches to Biblical themes.

A text was chosen (primarily by the well-meaning soul) for a Sunday night discussion in Fellowship Hall. The handful of people who came could be seen, immediately upon arrival, as members of what might be termed the "leftist" wing of the church, "leftist" in this case meaning "curious" or "open to new ideas." The "new idea" being explored in the chosen text (*Love Wins!* by Rob Bell) asserted that, underneath all of the Pauline doctrinal strictures in the New Testament, and all the stern laws of the Old Testament, lay Jesus's all-important concept of "love."

Disagreement with this notion was instantaneous.

"Seems rather soft-headed to me," declared a young man who had "once been a Presbyterian." "Jesus was about much more than love."

What else was He about, asked the woman sitting beside him.

"Well, think about all the tough messages in some of the parables," the young man countered. "And the time he flipped over the moneylenders' tables."

The conversation suddenly veered down a more exegetical path. "What kind of 'tough message' are you referring to?" asked another guest.

The man started to say something about the parable of the prodigal son, but interrupted himself to pursue a more urgent thought.

"We can't just love everyone and everything!" he exclaimed. "Christians have to stand for something!"

An older woman suggested that "love" motivated the two central commandments of the Sermon on the Mount, that "love" was something to stand for.

"Yes, but what does *that* mean?" he countered. "You can't 'love' murderers! You can't 'love' Islamic terrorists!" He paused and, wearing what he took to be a sly expression, turned to the group at large. "Tell me: how many of you *loved* Obama?"

People laughed hesitantly, but no hands were raised. Instead, what followed was the kind of silence which, in my little town, signals a breach of decorum. Notice, however, how quickly politics insinuated itself into a discussion about religion. Also, notice how quickly I will now change the subject, reserving the necessary discussion of politics in my little town until a bit later. I know how to quit when I'm ahead.

Mr. Nielsen

I don't know why I think using a pseudonym for the man I now write about will fool one single soul in my little town. I do know that Mr. Nielsen will recognize himself and be *very* put-out to read these comments. At least to a point. He prefers a selective sort of privacy, and for so public a figure, he wears his celebrity with an effacement that only partially obscures his pride in his many achievements and civic contributions. Board member at one time of almost every organization. Revered public high school instructor for more than forty-five years. Clear-voiced second tenor in the choir, beloved Sunday school leader, erstwhile pillar of the United Methodist Church. Renowned cook of "Southern country" cuisine. Gardener of the highest order. Expert maker of jams and jellies. Dedicated friend.

As a revered public school teacher, Mr. Nielsen also personifies much of what is good in my little town and its way of life. From Helen Keller's Annie Sullivan to Dumbledore in the *Harry Potter* series, we have read about them throughout literature, seen them in movies: those selfless men and women, steadfastly at their desks every morning, constantly refining lesson plans which they hope will inspire their students, offering suggestions that they hope will change lives and often do. Among these are the quiet leaders, the exemplars, the one who can be counted on to hold feet to the fire and stand up for what is right.

Mr. Nielsen is one of those teachers, and among its best virtues is the fact that my little town holds his gifts and service in high esteem. However, a saint he is not. (He would be the first to admit it.) He tolerates false adulation, let alone sentimentality, with a gimlet eye. He is a master contrarian. He can be rascally, stubborn, disagreeable, hilarious and caustic by turn. These adjectives might also describe his brothers—"the Nielsen boys" as they have been called even into their sixties and seventies—who are sure to add a dangerous zest to almost any gathering. (His "baby" brother Desmond, now in his sixties, has a notoriously waspish tongue. His salty exchanges with friends and foes have encased him in a crusty reputation that affords only a favorite few access to a man given to many secret acts of kindness.)

Born on a farm near Sprott, Alabama, a few miles from where Walker Evans took the photographs for *Let Us Now Praise Famous Men,* Mr. Nielsen is one of my own famous men. But his fame for me, his exceptionality, lies in what he has *not* done in his life. He has never flown on an airplane, never been north of Tennessee, never eaten nouvelle cuisine, never been to the ballet or opera, never gone to Europe, never been in a sailboat, never married, never done so many things that so many of us assume will be a part of our lives.

At the same time, he can grow a gorgeous flower garden, perform a clinical dissection of an English essay, whip up a delectable caramel cake, play a melodious "Abide by Me" on the piano, tell a story that will leave you in stitches, conquer a challenging hand of bridge, design a landscape engaging for even novice gardeners. His other talents are given to service, to making others shine. He will be at your door at 4 a.m. to take you to the hospital. He will help you host a large dinner party. He will bake cookies for your guests at Pilgrimage. If he feels like it, he will rake your yard without asking or expecting anything in return.

He is famous in my little town for all those things, and more. At the same time, he is also infamous, after retiring from his teaching career, for quitting part-time jobs or civic boards in a huff and writing Letters to the Editor of the *Times-Standard* that zing with corrective zeal. He is not without his fits and feuds and four-letter words when the occasion arises, which they often do. His dislikes run deep: Hillary Clinton, a sloppily mown lawn, a poorly weeded garden, "trifling" of any kind, bad grammar, "box" cakes, social posturing, too much Book of Common Prayer. ("All this *reading* you Episcopalians do!" he murmured to me once after a service. "It's enough to put you to *sleep*.")

From his farmer father he got a crafty sense of humor, a love of cigarettes, and a strong need for independence. From his mother, herself a schoolteacher and a formidable church pianist, he learned exactitude and an almost insolent self-confidence. Neither parent put up with any "shenanigans." Nor has he, particularly in the classroom, where he has cracked down hard on hundreds of students through the years, smacking the sides of a few heads and an occasional bum without any concern for political correctness or parental disapproval.

And yet, stroll across the town square with him and you'll hear outcries of "Hey, Mr. Nielsen!" or "I miss you, Mr. Nielsen!" from former students. At these moments, his face registers that same joy most talented teachers receive from the payback of students who loved them and were affected by their particular examples. Suddenly, his eyes twinkle, and he'll wave, and then mention a specific memory of the greeter.

"Oh, he was a dumb one!" he'll say, *sotto voce*, with a smile. "But a hard worker. Tried and tried and *tried* to learn to spell, but couldn't get his own name right to save himself!"

Or, "She was one of the good ones. Talked too much but had what it takes."

Or, "A no-account. Complete waste of space!" And then, undisturbed by his negative opinion, he'll wave back at the no-account, happy to be remembered and just as pleased the memory is shared.

Within these greetings, within the world that Mr. Nielsen inhabits with such ease, lies a mysterious, seemingly paradoxical, secret of life in my little town, discovered long ago by William Butler Yeats in *The Celtic Twilight*:

"In the great cities we see so little of the world, we drift into our minority. In the little towns and villages there are no minorities; people are not numerous enough. You must see the world there . . . Every man is himself a class . . ."

And, Yeats might have added, in these circumstances, every man is himself a gift.

Mr. Nielsen is just that: to the town, to his family, and to me.

Social Life

It's that time again. That special night again. The third Thursday of the month. The night of the Harmonie Club dinner!

You sigh and sigh again. Do you really have to go? The reasons you should attend serve as a nagging catechism: the reality of the social significance of the group; the fact that you were invited—and agreed—to join it; the horror that you are one of the co-hosts; the truth that you enjoy seeing many of the members.

The reasons you do not want to attend also flare up as the event approaches: you never quite seem to fit in; the conversation always seems to be the same; the cocktail hour is rarely long enough.

You make the "right" decision. Before you know it, you find yourself hefting a Coleman cooler up the steps of the Women's Seminary building. The cooler contains two large aluminum pans of the main course for the evening meal: chicken lasagna. (You didn't make it yourself.) You unlock the door, reviewing the table arrangements on your way to the kitchen. The theme for the evening is "April Showers"; accordingly, your co-host has found plastic bouquets for the centerpieces, each sporting a small Japanese umbrella, color-coordinated with the placemats and napkins.

You set up the bar. The Coleman cooler, full of ice from Food Value, will serve as the ice bucket, as well as the storage container for the white wine and, unless you catch the error in time, the red wine. (Red wine with ice cubes happens often enough in my little town to make commenting on it either a waste of time or unnecessarily fussy.) Spirits will be furnished as needed by the particular members who require them. Bourbon is a favorite (but not Southern Comfort—too sweet!), as is Scotch, and Seagram's 7, and, for a certain favorite colonel, gin. Soft drinks are preferred by the few Baptists among the group.

Concentrating on your work, you forget the time. Before you know it, 7 p.m. is here. The guests begin to trail in, wives bringing their choice of dish appropriate to their assigned category: salad, appetizer, side dish, dessert. You greet each attendee at the door, welcoming the college administrators, the retired colonels and lieutenant colonels, the large landowners, the leading businessmen, the college instructors, the retired judges, the retired teachers, the vicar, the veterinarian. All professionals, but few professional women. And no single women. And, without making an issue of it, no blacks. But one Muslim (married, assimilated). And one single man: me.

If there were a country club in my little town (and we used to have one, with a clubhouse), these men and women would be its stalwarts. We're a comfortable crowd, comfortable with our selves, comfortable with each other, comfortable in the large, open room. As we should be. As we *must* be, seeing each other as we do almost daily, everywhere: the hairdresser, the supermarket, the courthouse square, the doctor, the church. Many, many of the group are

Episcopalians, some Methodists, very few Baptists, two Jews, the last Jews in town.

The Baptists are few, by the way, not because of their lack of influence or their unacceptability but because of the acknowledgement that liquor is part of the evening agenda. Each Harmonie Club dinner begins with the suggestion of a cocktail hour—a "suggestion" because half of the crowd doesn't drink (at least in public) and the other half would like the gesture to be more extensive, more serious. (The cocktail "hour" becomes a cocktail half-hour on nights when couples who don't drink are hosting.)

Glancing around the room, you are reminded again of the average age of the members (sixty-five) and of your own mortality. As you ponder how old you are, you find yourself, as host, running back and forth, kitchen to bar, bar to tables, adding another set-up here, replenishing the beer there. Between tasks, you work in a few snatches of conversation, dialogue which almost always follows a script:

YOU: Hi, X. How *are* you?

X: Great. How are *you* (pronounced "yew")?

(There is a momentary pause here.)

X: How've you been?

YOU: Busy! There always seems to be too much to do. And you?

X: Oh, me too! There never seems to be enough time!

(Another pause, a longer one, long enough that you feel a need to direct the conversation.)

YOU: How are the grandkids?

X: (relieved, eager to talk) Oh, just great. We're going to visit them next week . . .

(At this point, if you are lucky, you will be called away to take care of another task. If you are less fortunate, you will work hard at continuing the dialogue until you actually are *called away.)*

The cocktail hour continues for a few more minutes, the men having formed one conversational group, the women another. The choice of conversational topics seems to repel the two genders from each other, and they inevitably end up in two large circles at opposite corners of the rooms. Suddenly, it is again 1855 and we are in a scene from *Jezebel!,* Bette Davis suggesting to the women at the dinner table that they "repair" to the parlor to let the men "do whatever our men do. Whatever do you suppose they talk about?!" (Easy answer: "our" men talk about local politics, crops, weather, Auburn or Alabama football games).

During these minutes, you notice that women have begun setting the serving tables, one for the main course, salads and side dishes, and a separate table for dessert. You offer to help but are quickly, if politely, brushed aside. Nor do you feel slighted at this dismissal, having learned as you live in Lovelady how capably these women can prepare an event, especially one focused on food. You have also learned that each of them (secretly) feels her skills in this area are superior to those of the others. A negotiation on placement of dishes or manner of service sometimes has the subtlety of a nuclear arms agreement and reveals the extent to which identities are constructed around an ability to *organize* a *meal.*

And how quickly the meal is organized! You call everyone to attention and, with your co-host, welcome them. Without being prompted, people grab hands and form a circle, a formation indicating intimacy, respect, inclusion. The blessing, carefully nondenominational but heartfelt, is delivered by the vicar, or if the vicar is absent, a Baptist deacon. A chorus of "Ah-mens" ("Ay-men" from the Baptists and Methodists) follows the blessing.

Dinner is served. *Bon appetit!* After everyone helps themselves from either side of the long serving table, you begin to relax, helping yourself to a plate and looking for a place to sit. You study the tables as discreetly as possible, looking for a seat beside the good storytellers, or the conversationally adept, or those young enough to still be able to hear you.

Sometimes your luck does not hold out long enough for you to make your way safely to your chosen chair. Someone—with the kindest of intentions—calls you over to sit next to Jim (deaf as a post) or Gloria (compulsive talker) or Betty (trapped in pleasantries). You obey. You sit down. You smile and endure, and then Florence, our chairwoman, clangs her spoon on a glass and asks that we sing "Happy Birthday" or "Happy Anniversary" to anyone being honored that month. Everyone applauds; there is a real joy in their faces as they wish each other well. But their faces also reflect fatigue. It is 8:30 p.m. and getting late for our group. (We are old and we get up early.) Flo announces the date of next month's Harmonie Club dinner, and the evening ends with a scraping of chair legs on the wooden floor and the affectionate good-byes of people who see each other every day, who have watched their children grow up, who have gone to too many funerals together.

Your evening—the host's evening—continues, however. You gather all the silverware and hand it in a basket to the next host to take home and wash. You collect the garbage. You pack up the bar and make sure that no one has forgotten a dish or a serving utensil. Alone in the big, open room, you look up occasionally as you finish your chores, watch the couples walking down the brick path through the dark night to their cars, the husband often walking ahead of the wife, who carries the half-empty serving dish. You review the evening, wishing you could have discovered more of the *meaning* of the lives of these kind men and women, and wondering how they could be so satisfied with their world, so consolidated in their political and religious perspectives.

Then, just as you are preparing to turn the key in the outside lock, here comes Cassie! She's in a mock tizzy, having forgotten her serving spoon. She locates the utensil, tosses off some pleasantries about a "senior" moment, and slips away into the starless night as a light rain begins to fall.

Cassie demands, and deserves, our attention. Tall, sixty-ish, hair always stylishly done in a flip or chignon, she is the attractive wife of one of the seven or eight families who own the most land in Huntley County, wield the most political influence, live in the grandest homes, count each others' families as "our kind" even as "our kind" disappears. These families appreciate their position in the society of my little town, a society which has remained determinedly feudal, having imported the manor house and its dependents from England, then switched the manor house for a plantation, and then converted the plantation into the present system based on patriarchal *noblesse oblige*. The rest of us, while not quite in thrall to these families, play at behaviors not dissimilar to those of people-in-waiting in a Carolingian court. We smile a little more broadly when we happen upon them in the grocery store, laugh a little more loudly at their jokes, allow them attitudes we would not accept in each other, recognize their achievements with a bit of extra praise.

And we play guessing games about them, gossip at a safe distance. How many acres does Cassie's family own—twenty thousand, thirty thousand? What is the name of Jane's two lifelong black household retainers? Tootie? Tempest? How much did the Staeblers spend on the renovation of their kitchen? (Rumor has the figure at $500,000, but that *can't* be correct.) And how is Willodeen's project coming along, the one designed to restore the old plantation village as a tourist destination?

The questions keep coming, but what's a little gossip among us serfs? It gets us through our days, keeps us focused on who really counts. These seven or eight families run most of the civic organizations and the churches and the farm-supported local businesses. They take pains to influence the decisions of the County Commission and City Council. Their names appear regularly in the *Times-Standard*. Without them, my little town would not exist, or at least would exist as a charmless backwater.

The children of these families endure a special set of challenges. Like the children of Britain's royal family, some would like to escape to the larger world, some would like to hide from the responsibilities of their positions, some happily embrace their significance and do their families proud. Among the latter group are the children who must worry about whatever future awaits my little town. To allay these worries, the children sometimes oversee initiatives intended to restore the civic glory, initiatives which start with great fanfare and often die out as quickly as sparklers.

The names of these efforts hold within themselves the golden dreams of my little town: Renaissance Lovelady, Main Street USA, the Dial and Discover Lovelady Audio Tour. Propping up these dreams are certain images: coaches packed with tourists visiting a restored mansion or two, then stopping to witness the spot where Jimmie Lee Jackson was shot; cute cafes on the courthouse square, travelers dining on stories of the dramatic strife embedded in the history of our little town; sidewalk traffic full to bursting with window shoppers looking for a memory purchase at one of the bustling antique stores. These fantasies persist through initiative after initiative, fueled by the same suspect vision: My little town as Plantation Land, its own Dollywood, finally getting a measure of "bang for the buck" by exploiting its past and manifesting it as theme.

The social life among blacks in Lovelady remains, to me at least, a mystery, as does the nature of their social structure. From my distant vantage point, I can deduce that a success in high school sports, years spent living in a Northern city, or anything to do with a divinity degree, seem to carry a certain clout. (The number of Lovelady ministers who aspire to political office, or hold political office, confirms the social power of black ministers, who are almost

always male.) On the only occasion I was invited to cross the color barrier and join a lawn picnic at the home of a black couple who had lived for years in New Jersey, I could feel the genuine attempt at outreach while also cringing at its self-conscious artifice.

"I know," the hostess murmured to me as dessert was served. "Watermelon. But I thought I'd skip the fried chicken. That would have been overkill." She laughed and poked me gently in the arm.

I know she meant her remark in good fun and that she could have gotten away with it further North, but, whether it was my unnerving minority perspective at the occasion or the brutal proximity of the site of Jimmy Lee Jackson's shooting directly across the street, I couldn't think of an appropriate response.

Women's Clubs

Lovelady loves its women's clubs, although not quite as much as it did a few decades ago. But just consider the number of these clubs still puttering along: the Garden Club, the Garden *Gate* Club (do *not* confuse the two), the Busy Bees, the Gadabouts, the Homemakers Club, the Prairie Women's Club, Episcopal Church Women, Methodist Church Women, Presbyterian Church Women, Baptist Women, Nazarene Women. The disproportionate number of these clubs not only reflects an earlier period in the history of my little town, a period of greater population and more money, but mirrors the strategies for influencing public policy many rural and small-town women throughout the country pursued in the early twentieth century, after World War I: a desire to effect change, to matter in what was so determinedly a man's world.

You can see this urge clearly in many of the efforts of Lovelady's women's clubs. Take the club project to restore the city cemetery and protect its graves and monuments. A local wife of a leading citizen initiated the project and helped it grow into a successful testament to the ability of a club to enhance civic life. With gentleness, she commandeered many in the community to support this effort.

119

Cadets from the military institute came on Saturday to mow and weed, joining Rinehart College volunteers and community boosters who understood the significance of what a cemetery's appearance implies about the health of my little town, and about the town's commitment to one of the most basic planks of our social platform: that we will honor our dead. This platform, this code, still matters in my little town, and the women's clubs uphold it fervently.

Then there are those understandable occasions when their meetings appear to be driven less by social codes than by a foraging for relevance. Or by a need to keep engaged, helpful. Sometimes, reading the minutes of these meetings in the "Lifestyle" page of the *Times-Standard*, you feel as though you are trapped in a "get-together" of the Thanatopsis Club, the women's club Sinclair Lewis savaged in *Main Street*, his jeremiad against small-town life. Occasionally, these minutes read as an unintentional signal to how little the role of Lovelady women has changed compared to that of their sisters in Atlanta or Dallas.

For example: On September 24 a few years ago, the Garden Club met at the Korner Kitchen for a luncheon buffet. A collect was given. Reports from the secretary and the treasurer were read, the latter showing a balance on hand of $479.48. Florence (the same Florence who chaired the Harmonie Club dinner) reported on a State of Alabama Garden Club meeting she attended in Birmingham. Her report was followed by a presentation on the benefits of composting.

"Much interest [about the presentation] was expressed," read the minutes, "and a good discussion on the experiences of members with the practice of composting [followed]."

Another example: At a January 19 meeting of the Three Arts Club a year later, the agenda concerned "this year's [club] theme—'Celebrating the Huntley County Great Outdoors.'" Doug Fields from the neighboring hamlet of Oak Hill "shared with us his love for honeybees and his honeybee business." Among the facts shared by Mr. Fields: a lighter color of honey has a milder taste and the darker color a stronger taste, and honey can be used to treat cuts, cold sores, fewer blisters, and sore throats. The report concluded that "The presentation was interesting, informative, and enjoyable."

I thought for some time after reading these minutes about the differences between those last three adjectives, finally realizing that, redundant as they might seem, they served as code for the values inherent among these clubs and the women who have kept them alive long after the larger society has declared them culturally obsolete.

To be "interesting" is to be considerate of your audience. (Nothing too complicated, in other words.)

To be "informative" is to share facts challenging insofar as they lie within the bounds of what passes for common sense.

And to be "enjoyable" is to address topics that support the way that life should be, that life is, that life will ever be.

You might ask why any woman in twenty-first-century America would seek membership in one of these clubs, why for some women in my little town an invitation to become a member of the Gadabouts is treasured almost as profoundly as a marriage or a childbirth. To pose this question, however, is to reverse the central point: the power of social exclusion in a town of three thousand

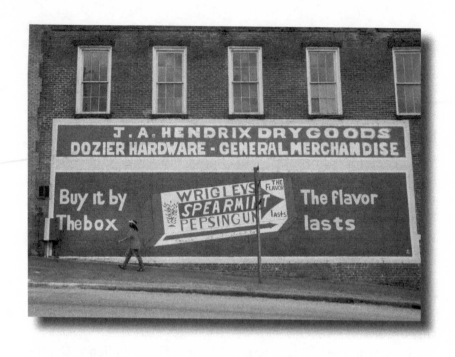

people can be painful, as can the degree of social isolation a woman might feel on the cloudy afternoon of the meeting of a club she has not been asked to join.

The hierarchy of prestige among these clubs further complicates issues of class and social mobility. Sitting atop the pyramid of these clubs, so securely that its members are hard-pressed not to show a certain smugness, is the Gadabouts. (All the wives of the first families are members of the Gadabouts.) Then comes the Busy Bees. (All the wives of the first families are also members of the Busy Bees.) Then comes the Garden Club, followed by the Garden Gate Club, followed by the Prairie Women's Club, the women's organizations of each church, and then all the rest.

Among the least prestigious of the women's clubs, a fact acknowledged by the bluntest of its members, is the Homemakers Club. Homemaker members are the new-to-town women, the single women, the single *professional* women, the women whose husbands have lower-echelon positions in the colleges. Somehow, despite their reduced status, these women keep their heads high, contributing to the health of the commonweal, getting together on a monthly basis, traveling to some new place or listening to some new speaker or spending time in some earnest activity such as "scrapbooking," and in doing so improve the town's lot smidgen by smidgen.

While the women are busy with their clubs, the men of my little town avoid even the *thought* of organizing a club. (They used to have a few service clubs—Rotary, The Serviteers among them—but all have since died out as the memberships dwindled.) Of course, Lovelady's men don't need to worry about effecting change. At least in name, they already have all the social influence, all the economic power, all the control. And although we are still living in something of a patriarchy in Lovelady, the role of our men hides an irony well known to the natives. Despite their public postures, the men of my little town privately defer to their wives in many matters, social and otherwise. "Steel magnolias" is not an expression invented without cause.

Conversation

The joy I receive from listening to the conversation of the citizens in my little town confuses them. It sometimes confuses me, because my pleasure in hearing them shows (extravagantly) on my face and in my unsettling (to them) degree of enthusiasm at their use of language. So intent am I on catching the lexical twists, the sly humor, the offbeat silences, the sultry pace, the anecdotes so cannily structured as to appear pre-planned, that, when they pause and look at me, indicating it's *your* turn, *say something*, I get caught off-guard and find myself staring at them blankly.

What do I hear in the words framed by those stretched vowels and soft "r" sounds and sense of dramatic license? Why am I not similarly in thrall to the dialects of New England, of London? Certainly, in those more familiar locales, the topics might be higher-minded, the range of reference more widely framed, the facts declared with more logical support. But only in my little town do I hear conversation as music.

If conversation can be thought of in these terms, as many have, then the discourse of New England might be the equivalent of Bach: densely contrapuntal, sonorous, with an occasional reference to another key for a twist of color and surprise. The discourse of London? Ineffably Beethoven, with deft modulations, an architectonic control of themes, and a vocabulary full of juxtapositions, multiple switches in keys and motifs.

But in my little town? We're safely in the land of Edward Kennedy "Duke" Ellington, enjoying the verbal counterpart to his uncalculated, devil-may-care rhythms, his ever-present awareness of the blues, his smooth-then-harsh vocalizations of emotion, and his jig-sawed musical references, as diverse as Cotton Club razz-ma-tazz and the "jungle growl" of stride bass patterns.

There remains one slight difference from Ellington: the conversation in my little town firmly refuses to stoop to the genteel, allowing tales to include the occasional expletive, the sly reference to a body part, and an open-armed dismissal of ordinary anecdotal pace. I've heard "jokes" go on for as much as thirty minutes without interruption, listeners rapt, the speaker languidly strolling through the narrative, pausing to meander up a path of side-story here, then a lengthy description there, never worried about audience attention. Their secret? Seeming to go nowhere can lead you just where you wanted to go all along.

Many of the anecdotes in my little town are based on family life, or civic life, and because of this close cultural embrace between speaker and listener, any pressure to worry about being understood or appreciated evaporates as surely as the morning dew on a gardenia. No subject needs to be explained or avoided. The topic can be a favorite coon dog, the time Uncle Chester got stuck in the outhouse, when a drunken William Faulkner came to speak in the Chapel, a drug bust on The Hill, or the unduly décolleté bridesmaid outfits at Lulu's wedding.

The significance of this uniform perspective echoes an earlier period in our cultural history (some would say the 1950s, others the period before World War I) and gives conversation in my little town a self-reinforcing validity and sure-footedness. This harmony is especially true when it comes to humor. Significantly, humor in the form of metaphors. Metaphors require an understanding of the items being compared and then a further understanding of what holds the two items in common. Metaphors, by implication, require a common culture.

Some of the favorite expressions using metaphor in my little town:

It happened faster than a knife fight in a phone booth.

He couldn't carry a tune if he had a bucket with a lid on it.

That's about as useful as a trap door on a canoe.

He's busier than a one-legged man at an ass-kickin' contest.

Somebody beat him with an ugly stick.

If you don't quiet down, I'm goin' to slap the taste right out of your mouth.

I'll slap you up 'side the face so hard you'll see tomorrow today.

He's so thin he has to stand up twice to cast a shadow.

That boy makes about as much sense as tits on a tree.

Can you understand why someone from the North Shore of Boston might find any conversation which includes this appreciation of image, a (relatively) shocking mix of language registers, and such refreshingly brutal truths, worth careful listening?

And finally, in a graphic example of the belly-laugh a little misspelling can bring, my favorite bit of local humor, seen driving down County Road 24 one afternoon on my way to Centreville. A large handcrafted sign was posted in the front yard of a trailer: *"Ho Made Apple Butter!"*

Down the road one hundred feet, at the next trailer, another sign had been posted:

"She did what?"

Now if that don't beat all, I don't know whether to scratch my watch or wind my behind.

Race

If only the fenced-off public swimming pool in my little town could talk. Its empty blue rectangle, so barren and reproving next to the sparkling water tower on Pickett Street, would tell stories full of the same seemingly ineradicable social prejudices that prevented a swimming pool from being built in the middle of New York's Central Park in 1910 and in 2015 provoked a group of white adults at a private community swimming pool in McKinney, Texas, to tell a group of black teens to "go back to your Section 8 homes."

These insurmountable biases are identical to those that caused my little town's swimming pool to rust, to corrode, to remain a testament to sad, defeating racial divides that have existed here for hundreds of years. Although public swimming pools were formally desegregated after the civil rights movement, most Southern cities and towns shut down their public pools rather than permit mixed-race swimming.

My little town follows the pattern. Residents will tell you that the pool remained open for a few summers after it was dug in the middle 1990s. During these few months, to everyone's credit, there were no outright arguments or fights in or around the pool—perhaps because so few whites used it.

Without fanfare, however, the whites who did swim there quickly withdrew, adopting the strategy so often employed in these cases: retreat to a safe zone, be it to the suburbs or a country club or to a private school. And so alternative "community" pools appeared in various spots around Huntley County, at which white members paid annual dues just high enough to allow entrance to only the most "suitable" residents.

When asked about the pool on Pickett Street, few people still remember its demise, or are willing to talk about it. By inference, when they are asked, one can gather from the frequent mentions of "different cultures," that the blacks "behaved" differently at the swimming pool than did whites. Meaning: the music from their radios and tape players was too disturbing, their conversation too animated and insistent to achieve any possible state of relaxation associated in some cultures with "sitting by the pool." Meaning: all those screaming children, running, jumping, ignoring the customary protocol of pool usage. Meaning: so many inches of well-oiled black skin so near to you, floating in the water, sweating in the water.

To be fair, one of these arguments has some merit, insofar as blacks socializing together often seem to produce noise to a degree not usually heard among groups of whites (except at a football game). And, to reverse the argument, blacks have their own convincing rationales for their unfettered boisterousness: they often see white get-togethers as duller than dirt, hampered by tired conversation and boring choices in music and food. You call *that* fun?

Which brings us to the fundamental disagreement about what constitutes appropriateness in the most basic public behaviors in my little town. Why did I not write at greater length about the many black friends I have made in my more than a decade here? Because they do not make themselves available for friendship. Why no interesting stories about black social life? Because I have so rarely experienced it.

For more than a decade here the blacks have for me remained a mystery, often living quietly in the woods outside the city limits of my little town, along the county roads in old trailers. Interracial events are gamely attempted again and again, only to peter out without apparent reason or any clear hostility from those who just don't show up. The implicit message (from many blacks) remains: leave us alone. We don't seek your company. *We get along without you very well.*

The whites often respond in kind. As an example of this message, consider Halloween, once our most predictable of holidays. The Halloween of my youth centered around a specific routine: you put on your costume, you visited the neighbors, you "surprised" the person at the door with a shy "Trick or Treat," you identified your costume, you opened your goodie bag, you got your goodies, you thanked your Halloween host, and you went on your way, comparing your treats with those of your companion tricksters.

However. In my little town, Halloween manifests itself as just the kind of exercise in inter-cultural avoidance in which we seem to specialize. Not always, not *every time,* but often enough to merit a mention,

In other words, the holiday as practiced in my little town defies my expectations. My first Halloween here, I followed my usual customs, buying enough candy corn and Reese's Pieces and "Fun-Sized" Twix and bags of Kit-Kat bars to satisfy an eager horde of princesses and pirates. How naïve I was. Even before I had turned on my front porch light at 5:30 p.m., cars were pulling up and idling at the end of my sidewalk on Lee Street, parents waiting behind the wheel while back doors flew open and children spilled onto the sidewalk, racing toward the front door.

I stood there, wearing the expression of mock Halloween "horror" worn by adults in this moment everywhere. More and more cars pulled up. More and more children raced down the sidewalk. Few, if any, of the children wore even the suggestion of a costume. A little late in the game, I understood the point: the holiday as practiced here, the point of *their* holiday, had little to do with imagination, the fun of being someone else. Most of them did not even think to say "Trick or Treat" because they felt little need for the sweet Halloween role-playing that had always, to me, seemed integral. They were here for one reason only: the candy. Each stood before me with a full-sized paper grocery bag, staring up at me, saying nothing, waiting for the bag to be filled. After handing out some candy, along with an apple as healthy ballast, I said "Happy Halloween" and waved them off to the next house.

But they didn't move. Their bags remained open, their faces resentful. "More!" one or two of them said. "More! And no apples!" I explained, slowly and clearly, lessons about sharing—that I had to save some treats for the next visitors—and, after some moments of impatience on both of our parts and not a little reluctance on theirs, they left the porch, clearly dissatisfied with their haul.

After three of these visits, my treats were gone, my apples a memory, but still the cars kept pulling up. In defense, and embarrassment, I closed the front door and shut off the porch light. As I did so, I noticed that the porches of all of my neighbors, usually so well-lighted and welcoming, were dark.

The next day I recounted my experience to a woman who lived across the street.

"Oh, dear," she said. "I should have told you. It's sad, but you really can't celebrate Halloween here like you're used to doing. I haven't turned my porch light on for Halloween in the last five years."

None of the children who came to my door that first Halloween were white. Apparently, those white children had already celebrated their Halloweens—the one that I grew up with—in their white schools or white churches or white neighborhoods. Elsewhere. Behind closed doors.

Imagine how difficult, how inconvenient, acknowledging, let alone validating, this message of cultural avoidance can be when you're living side by side. The derisory tut-tutting about "the racial divide in the South" so common among Northerners is usually seen here as hopelessly naive.

"But they're not like your blacks up North—assimilated, educated," was the explanation given to me by a man who grew up on a thousand-acre farm in nearby Dallas County. "They're just a few generations off the plantation."

And so going to the Walmart in nearby Selma, a store used predominantly by blacks, is seen by some white friends as "unpleasant," "threatening." And so outreach between black and white churches fails with a sad frequency. When I attended a black church one Sunday to enjoy the singing, people smiled at me, but smiled strangely, as though they could not quite comprehend why I was there.

Any attempt to conceive of possible solutions to this degree of social segregation ends in shrugged white shoulders and fatalistic expressions of regret. (*That's just the way they are.*) Most blacks will not even talk about the segregation; the few who do cannot get beyond their anger.

But then many people in my little town seem angry, resentful, nursing a well-developed sense of victimhood. And their anger comes back, so often, to the "race issue." To mention the original version of this issue—slavery—is to annoy the whites ("Can't we just put that behind us?"). To act as if this sin has been atoned for is to inflame the blacks. (It will never be atoned for.) Why? Because the roots of the issue go back more deeply than a few decades, far more deeply, beginning with the importation of the West Indian slave state to Charleston, and then transferring it throughout the Deep South, bringing along with it a fierce racial dominance dependent on total obedience and enforced by means of civil and political brutality.

Can you feel the righteous anger? On both sides? Despite the Voting Rights Act and the Civil Rights Act and Head Start and Medicaid and SNAP and all the other social programs instituted since 1964, the blacks are angry, deservedly so, at how difficult a time they, as sixty percent of the population, have had in gaining a foothold on the comparative privilege possessed so assuredly by their white neighbors.

The whites, the "forgotten" people so unswervingly loyal to a recent president, are angry too, deservedly so, for the same reason (jobs in the "new" economy are no more available to them than to their black brethren), and for two others, in their minds: their ruined—but integrated!—public education system and the wasteful, initiative-destroying, largesse of government checks received by the blacks. (Never to be acknowledged is the reason so many checks are cut by the government: the traditional ladder of opportunity is missing a few rungs, namely the rungs where one finds jobs that pay a living wage.)

This was supposed to be my time, whites (especially uneducated whites) seem to be saying. *But, because of you blacks, it is not.*

For despite all the checks and all the highly engineered integration, little in my little town is integrated, except maybe at the Lovelady Clinic, where the dedicated but overworked doctor and nurse clinicians treat all comers with equal care. But dedication can only do so much. The medical treatment for the rural poor remains segregated by income and unemployment. Only a few years ago, a national magazine came to report on the tuberculosis outbreak in my little town and, in a well-researched article entitled "Where Health Care Won't Go," chronicled this particular niche of inequality. (The poverty rate among blacks in Huntley County is three times that of whites.)

You cannot get away from race in my little town. *I* cannot get away from race among my own reasons for living here. I remained unaware of this ugly fact until years after I arrived. Truth: I am no better than anyone else when it comes to using blacks as the modern version of slaves. I use them not as egregiously as slaves were once used, but the economic system—the class system—in my little town encourages a contemporary, only slightly milder, version of the same abuse.

Besides a need for less urbanity and fewer people, I moved here in small part to secure affordable home care for an aging parent, "affordable" because I was told this care could be provided cheaply by the same black women whose grandmothers and great-grandmothers would have performed similar services in the Big House in the antebellum South. Additionally, I could have never hoped to keep up my foolishly large home without black "help." Although I pay more per hour to Mr. Thomas than would many of my neighbors (and I do this to their muted but heartfelt disapproval), I would pay triple or quadruple the per-hour rate to a white resident who performed the same electrical, plumbing, or painting services.

Further, could the original builders of my home have afforded the intricate woodworking, the coffered ceilings, without black men to create them? Am I not living in yet another, albeit more subtle, version of the West Indian slave state? And isn't the answer to that question obvious?

These thoughts can keep you up at night staring at the fourteen-foot ceilings in the bedrooms. Often, my thoughts turn to Thomas and my relationship with him. Ah, Thomas. Mr. Thomas. Gifted, handsome, father of a handful of children by different mothers. Still with the track-star physique which propelled him to victory in all those high school races. Still with the beautiful eyes—and still with the teeth rotted from years of absent dental care. Thomas. Sometimes available for work, sometimes in jail due to non-payment of child support. Whom I wish I could buy a house for, feed his children, stop him from trifling with his life.

I once asked him why he had not gone on to college. (He had been a relatively good student, according to one his teachers.)

He looked at me like I was the craziest of white men.

"No money, Mr. David. My mother had eleven children."

But there were scholarships, I argued. There were *ways*.

He picked up a hammer and started repairing the railing of the back porch, declining to say another word.

Often, the history of race in my little town complicates the simplest gestures between Thomas and me. Do we shake hands when we meet? Pat each other on the back? Should we touch at all and how would that be interpreted? To what degree should I inquire about his family without seeming overly solicitous or patronizing? How can I ever capture that intricate, historically practiced, intimacy that my white neighbors, raised in my little town, have established with their "help"?

But I can't think of Thomas as "help." That's the problem. He who will come on a Sunday (when no one else will) to see if he can fix a broken water heater. He who will—without asking—watch over a close friend who is dying, he who will surprise me with a repaired lawn mower. He who tolerates my picky demands and my strange English with a noble patience. (Although he denies doing so, I'm sure he changes his pronunciation and vocabulary when he speaks to me.)

He, who, with one kind gesture, can make me feel as if reparations are not such a bad idea.

Politics

One fact to remember about politics in my little town, located in the middle of the Black Belt: here (where blacks are in the majority), districts go blue, while the rest of Alabama remains a deep scarlet.

Another fact to consider: in 2015, the state enacted a law requiring photo identification to vote and then promptly closed the Department of Motor Vehicles offices in Black Belt counties. A federal investigation confirmed that this targeting amounted to voter discrimination.

A final fact: My little town has a special asterisk attached to its history. It is the birthplace of the American version of the Kenyan-inspired "Barack Obama Day," a political observance in honor of the former President. Considering the demographics of the Black Belt, it is an appropriate birthplace. Obama Day, instituted on January 26, 2009, six days after President Obama's inauguration, has become a unique tradition here and a cause of parades and barbecues.

For the blacks. For the local whites, the occasion is seen quite differently. They scrupulously avoid the downtown area where the parade is held and comment, sometimes in Letters to the Editor, about the refuse left on the street and the courthouse lawn after the event is finished. They see the former President as a horrible ghost over our country's recent history, symbolizing the final up-ending of the segregated minority which had dominated the town for centuries.

Not coincidentally, County Commissioner Jack "Tiny" Thompson Jr, whom many credit as the guiding force behind the holiday, has become something of a symbol, as well. His is a name newcomers to my little town will hear frequently upon arrival, much more than that of his father, civil rights leader Jack Thompson Sr., who led the mule wagon that carried the body of the Rev. Dr. Martin Luther King Jr. at his funeral. "Tiny," as he is usually referred to by the local whites (never "Mr. Thompson") was most notoriously known as a leading supporter of the economic benefits of the dumping in a Huntley County landfill of four million tons of Kingston, Tennessee, coal ash, a toxic waste which carries mercury, lead, arsenic, and a dozen other heavy metals.

"We are on our way up," announced Thompson in one of his contemporary weekly broadcasts for WRAC-radio, referring to the windfall resulting from the purchase. "Glory be to God that we was able to hit this landfill deal and hit this coal ash."

Imaginative as it is to attribute a common purpose to God's blessings and fuel waste, Mr. Thompson's quote might have more to do with Lord Acton's maxim "Absolute power corrupts absolutely" than to rhetorical finesse. "Tiny," whose grandfather was a share-cropper, has dominated the politics of my little town since he was elected to the Huntley County Commission in 2000; he has been reelected for four subsequent six-year terms. He is hated, not always along racial lines, but because his strong civic presence represents a revolution of the town's governance, from the dominance of a sometimes corrupt white minority to that of a sometimes corrupt black majority. (So radical was this change, inspired in part from well-organized voter registration drives among black voters in the 1990s, that allusions to voter fraud are commonplace among whites after almost any local election in my little town.)

"What good does it do me to vote?" white friends will remark, referring to the lopsided victory of a black candidate. "Might as well whistle into the wind."

From this perspective, many of Mr. Thompson's efforts while on the Commission have been self-promoting, wrong-headed, or bent on directing any funds resulting from the passage of a motion toward the interests of "his" constituency.

There was, as has been mentioned, his very personal, and successful, drive toward instituting Obama Day.

There was his championing, and the subsequent 2004 Commission approval, of a private prison for Huntley County, one now located just off the town square, next to the old prison. The $20 million facility was touted as the harbinger of great potential economic benefits to the County. Those benefits have not, in any material way, appeared.

There was his enthusiasm for, and the Commission's subsequent 2012 approval, of a lease for a hotel/motel in Lovelady. The need for such an accommodation was inarguable, but my little town's ability to sustain such a venture seemed an incidental concern to the commissioners. As a result, the Quiet Nite Inn, which sits on the fringe of the Lovelady Golf Course, maintains a low rate of occupancy for most of the year and is regularly reported to be in financial trouble or on the verge of closing.

There was Commissioner Thompson's enthusiastic approval of the landfill appropriation, the money from which does not seem to have made its way onto the city streets or into the city schools.

There was Mr. Thompson's seemingly incomprehensible support for Jeff Sessions for Attorney General of the United States, a support which prompted his mother to speak out publicly in disagreement with her son.

There was the harassment suit instigated against Mr. Thompson by Ms. Ethel Collins. In the suit, Ms. Collins, one of the most unforgettable characters of my little town, not only expressed umbrage that Tiny had called her and others who opposed the coal ash landfill "hanky-headed niggers," but also that he "[had grabbed] her and [held] her to the ground."

These incidents continually crop up around Mr. Thompson's public persona, which, through his self-reverential civic appearances and his combative behavior in County Commission meetings, seems to his white constituents a parody of grandiosity. Nor did the webpage which appeared online in the autumn of 2010 (since removed) alter this impression. One photo in particular boldfaced his self-image. Wearing a lavender polo shirt, Mr. Thompson could be seen in a traditionally "presidential" pose, sitting behind a highly polished oversized desk. As there was already an official Commission web page with minutes and pictures of all commissioners, many saw this additional piece of self-promotion as *de trop*.

But, you might ask, isn't this to be expected? After centuries of

enslavement, why wouldn't the blacks in my little town misman-
age their access to a bit of local power? Could they be blamed for
overplaying their own part in political inequality, smashing aside
any efforts at ethical niceties or compromise? Shouldn't their wish
to direct money toward their own interests be seen as an expected,
if unhappy, part of human nature?

Perhaps. From the perspective of the local newspaper, however,
embrace of power is not quite the same as corruption of the local
body politic. The front page of the white-owned and edited *Times-
Standard* regularly features reports on County Commission meetings,
during which threats of physical violence seem almost *du jour*. And,
at least during the years an intrepid young reporter, John Allen
Clark, wrote many of the articles and editorials, the paper spoke
truth to this new power with a megaphone.

Mr. Clark is gone, however, and now, expressing their uncomfort-
ably minority perspective, the editorials of the paper have retreated
to a more nuanced view, resorting to a relatively resigned attitude
on some of the local problems and applying their opinions to a
national context, mixing issues such as politics and religion with
the ease of a child busily finger-painting.

The "Insight and Opinion" page of the weekly paper was for
years dominated by "From Where I Sit," a column written by the
company president, Mr. Bob Tribble. Beside Mr. Tribble's column
was "Reflections By: Michael J. Brooks," an ordained Baptist minister
who used his few inches of copy to apply the teachings of St. Paul to
relevant contemporary dilemmas, often from the author's own life.

Similarly, Letters to the Editor in the *Times-Standard* address not

142

so much a specific local issue as they do a complaint or warning or pleading about society in general:

An excerpt from one letter, dated June 6, 2013:

Human Right #1: We are all born free and equal! ... [Lovelady] has always been the seat of intelligence and I'm committed to Huntley County and the City of Lovelady. Let's go beyond the metaphoric stage and enjoy Life, Liberty, and the Pursuit of Happiness.

A letter from April 4, 2012:

There are four areas [of life] that should be addressed when raising children:

1. The Home, taught obedience, morals, responsibility, respect, etc.

2. The Church, take them [children] to church. This is where they learn about Jesus and the Christian way of living.

3. School, starting with pre-school. This helps to prepare them for the present and for the future ...

4. The World, if they're not taught at Home/Church/School, the world will teach them. And, believe me, it's a jungle out there if they're not prepared to face it.

And another, from Mr. Robert Nielsen, dated February 2, 2011:

... Since Tiny [Commissioner Thompson] is always castigating the "white folk," I'd like to take this opportunity to tell him that, from my many walks around the town, that it is not "white folk" trashing [a particular] site or in the alley behind the liquor store and the Department Store. I am sorry to admit that some of those doing the trashing are former students of mine. I thought that I had taught them to throw their garbage in a trash can, even if I was unsuccessful in teaching them anything about English.

Human rights. Child-rearing. Church-going. Littering. From these letters, and from the editorials, the world looms as "a jungle," dangerous, evil, trashed, forgetful of human rights, human decency. The world represents original sin. The world—well, here are some random sentences from various "From Where I Sit" columns:

... Newspapers, television, networks, and magazines have been outrageously abusive, untruthful, arrogant, and hypocritical ... (11/28/12)

...We Americans who oppose abortions must do all that we can to keep our tax dollars from funding something that takes the life of an unborn child ... (2/2/11)

... Seems that we have allowed some of these [national] foundations established by our forefathers to crumble away by electing people on the national level who do not appear to have a strong faith in God ... (11/24/10)

... Those of us who live in small communities are citizens of our state, nation, and world too; therefore, our opinions should be heard on these issues, as well as on local issues ... (1/15/11)

...political correctness rose to an outrageous level in [last year's] Fort Hood massacre ... (3/23/11)

... It seems we can no longer manage the world that God created ... If hope and change is our thing we should think about putting our hope in the Creator who made this world. If we need to change our way of living to please Him, then let's do it. Again. He made the world and we have allowed it to become a mess. God is really the only answer ... (3/23/11)

From this degree of alarm, it is only a short hop to an even more extreme level of concern, one that might lead you to vote for a figure you might ordinarily think immoral and unethical. Your level of concern, dominated by a seductive nostalgia and a cherry-picked religious faith, might provoke a convenient sidelining of your conscience in the name of political gain.

If only we could go back to the way things used to be. If only we could make America great again.

This point of view was championed as a slogan by a figure whom the writers of these columns trim their sails by. This figure said, during his election campaign, that he felt similarly besieged by "the world" (he called it "globalism") and promised to, while making America great again, save the nation from that world as *only he could.*

Our local "white" politics is a homegrown version of his cosmology, while our local "black" politics struggles to throw off the practices and principles of the "white" politics. And round and round we go. What else is there to say? Stuck in a cycle of competing angers, the political life in my little town is at a stalemate, riddled with mistrust, unsure of solutions, spun along by its historical ghosts.

Jews

My little town has, historically, appreciated its Jews, admired their business skills, agreed with their commonsensical approach to civic issues, dined with them, laughed with them, played golf with them, ignored any noticeable differences of faith. Curiously, this failure to make a social or theological issue of the major radical distinction between Judaism and Christianity—that Jesus was not divine—bears no similarity to the harsh intolerance toward each other witnessed among the various Protestant denominations of my little town. "They don't really practice Christianity," the pastor of one of the Baptist churches is said to have remarked about the small Episcopalian congregation. "I'm not sure what they believe."

Nonetheless, included as they are, Jews have almost disappeared here, as my little town disappears. The Skolnicks, purveyors of fine men's clothes, left in the 1950s, as did the Goldblatts. The last of the Schillers, Miss Bessie, died a decade ago. Boy Gene and Girl Jean Harris (as they are fondly referred to) closed their dry goods store in 2015, and their children have moved away. They are the last known Jews in town.

No more Jews! What will that mean to my little town? What did living there mean to them? What must it have been like when you have no synagogue, no formal acknowledgement of your holidays? What must it still be like, to live, as the writer Midge Decter lived growing up Jewish in a small flyover town, "perpetually between the hammer and the anvil, so constricted by the experience that to this day not a single serious Jewish novelist has risen from [Southern] literature to tell about [the experience]."

Charitably, the few Jews still living in my little town have exhibited a Christ-like degree of patience. Everyone undertakes Christmas and Easter here with an embrace of festivity—and with barely a glance at Hanukkah and Passover. Festivity as street decorations. As family events. As church services. How many Stars of Bethlehem can you hang from each street lamp at least thirty days before the Nativity? (Scores.) How many Christmas cantatas can you fit into Holy Week in December? (One for each church.) And so Jews must assimilate to a degree unheard of in coastal cities—or else live as outsiders, or else flee.

In my little town, they seem to have chosen the latter option, as they have in many small towns in Alabama. In fact, Dothan, Alabama, a cross-state city, understands the contributions of Jews to its civic life to the extent in 2013 of making the bold offer to provide Jews up to $50,000 to relocate there. (The contract included a five-year habitation stipulation.) Dothan understands, even by implication, that the economic vitality, the business acumen, the cultural inclusion, that Jews often bring to a town are irreplaceable. And to live without them, to try and "wish" them back again, will not happen quickly or easily here. Why would they ever return?

The Ghosts of Pilgrimage

I'm caught with no escape, back stiff with anticipation, all dressed up in a coat and tie in my living room and with no place to go. My palms are sweating. I can hear people coming up the sidewalk and approaching the front door, more and more of them, hear them laughing, chattering, coming up the steps, impatiently standing in line, waiting for Lillian to collect their tickets between sips from her "iced tea," a screwdriver hidden in a styrofoam cup. The doorbell rings. My eyes dart everywhere, my mind jerks from thought to thought. Have I forgotten anything? Are the appropriate candles lighted? Did I remember to put the "No Entry" sign on the door of the room where I've dumped everything I don't want anyone to see?

And what about the degree of persnickety-ness of the strangers who will walk through the rooms I live in every day, judging the *étagères*, the hall trees, the balloon-back dining chairs, the barrister bookcases, the pier mirrors, the marble fireplace mantles, the center tables and parlor tables, the *jardinières* and *secretaires*, the "Oriental" rugs, all the accumulated (and pointless) vanity of ten years' collecting of Victoriana?

Better question: Why do I put myself through this agony, beyond an inability to say "No"? Whom am I trying to impress? My home isn't really all that much, as I take a look around it, opening the door and letting a group of Pilgrimage visitors push into my quiet life, inspecting, evaluating, appraising, assessing. And I certainly don't get paid for doing this. (Monetarily, it's a losing proposition.)

And haven't I known better—and for so many years—ever since 1977, living in a tiny Greenwich Village walk-up, lying on my shabby convertible couch and laughing at an article a friend had written for the *New York Times* about her visit to the famous Pilgrimage of Natchez, Mississippi? The event seemed so exotic back then, so "Southern" and distant from my experience. I would never, certainly, find myself in the middle of *that* kind of occasion.

How funny life is. But no more time for rumination. They're coming in thick and fast now. I summon whatever charm I have, smiling excessively as I show visitors where to put a purse or introduce them to the first of the many "room" docents, those women (usually) who lead guests through the artifacts, throwing in bits of family history or stories of provenance. Some of the stories are true, some terribly dolled up, but the guests gush over them and gander at the bibelots, all excepting an architectural historian, who is challenging the docent on a factual error while ensuring that the immediate bystanders are aware of the fraud.

As well as its veneer of historicity, Lovelady's Pilgrimage has at its core that familiar American fascination with expensive real estate. We actually call our Pilgrimage the "Home Tour," a more honest moniker to indicate the often desperate desire of many tour hosts to promote a sale of their grand house, sales that are proving almost impossible to effect. So the occasion provides a unique opportunity for many buyers and sellers: a chance to show off and a chance to view real estate opportunities in a soft-sell circumstance which prettily masks a more venal purpose.

Also included in this $35-per-person opportunity is the same urge, albeit on a much smaller scale, that sends carloads of visitors gawking at the castles of Newport, the estates of the Main Line or Bel Air or Burlingame or Bronxville or Mountain Brook. This urge can be seen on the faces of the women and men coming through my front door. Their expressions speak of a similar envy. A guest has just asked me to write down the name of the paint color I used on my dining room walls. Another wants to know who renovated my bathroom.

I might be more susceptible to smugness at this degree of attention if I actually had renovated the home myself. Or had a staff commensurate with the size of the house. However, although the children of slaves or slaves themselves had everything to do with building my home and many of the homes on the Pilgrimages all over the South, these staffs disappeared after the Civil War as quickly as those in Edwardian homes after World War I.

As part of my hosting duties, I circle the house every half hour, checking to see if there is enough toilet paper in the bathrooms, if the punch bowls are filled. I am not surprised that the bowl of "Baptist" punch—the one without liquor—remains almost full, while the Fish House Punch, a few glasses of which once prompted my over-served mother to perform a perfect cartwheel in the bar of Bookbinder's Restaurant in Philadelphia, is almost gone. The cheese straws, the pimento cheese finger sandwiches, the hot chicken salad, have disappeared as quickly as January snowflakes on my front lawn.

Days pass, or so it seems, as I welcome and bid farewell to guest after guest, thanking them for their kind words, finding forgotten purses, answering questions, feigning interest in the long anecdote told to me by a descendent of the man who built my home. As his story ends, I look out the window of the butler's pantry to see that the light is fading. I excuse myself to turn on the lamps in the main rooms for the few people still wandering about. I can see that even the docents are winding down, looking worn and sounding mechanical as they recite their room descriptions.

At almost six o'clock in the evening, after six hours of entertaining almost three hundred strangers, the Pilgrimage—my Home Tour—is over. Or almost over. One last guest, a woman of significant proportions, has taken over a Morris chair in the living room. As I approach her, she is dabbing her handkerchief on a spot on the upholstery.

She looks up guiltily. "I'm so sorry," she explains. "I got careless. But that *punch*! It's so good I couldn't help but have a second cup!"

Farewell

Rarely have the dead been given a setting more appropriate for eternal repose than the Garden of Confederate Rest, seventy-seven faded and nameless headstones memorializing a cause some in my little town still revere. Their solemn message promotes itself most seductively in the late spring, when the blooms famous in the Deep South put on an insistent display as they flutter in the warm breeze.

One could—I do often—get lost in all this pastoral splendor. On this particular afternoon, the dogwood trees furnish a white backdrop for the heartache blue of the hydrangeas, the screaming pink of the camellias, the bloody scarlet of the azaleas. Lying beside a redwood tree planted in honor of the sacrifice of these dead soldiers, I find it easy to think those grand thoughts—about death, about the passage of time—that cemeteries are famous for invoking. And I find myself remembering my original purpose for coming to my little town, the challenge which opened this book: Have I found a home here? Or am I just another Odysseus, facing a riddle similar to that confronted by the ancient Greek wanderer in the W. S. Merwin poem:

... There were the islands
Each ... to be navigated, and one to call "home."
... And what wonder
If sometimes he could not remember ...
which, improbable, remote, and true,
Was the one he kept sailing home to?

For a decade I have thought of these three thousand people as my home, improbable, remote, yet true. I have tried to disappear into my little town, never again to worry about where I would finally finish, how I would be buried, who would mourn me.

But the possessive adjective remains a mockery. My little town does not seem "mine" at all, even now, even after all these years. Even after we have grieved together, prayed together, laughed to-gether, drunk together.

But why not? What's missing? What part of "home" does the town not fulfill? And is it the town's fault? Or mine?

When answering these questions, I am giving something up, admitting a secret I had hoped to hide. Up to this moment, I had wanted to avoid admitting that I despise too much of what makes the people of my little town fit so perfectly into it. I do not admire that they refuse to know, and to imagine, so much of the world. I do not admire their ways of making me uncomfortable talking about whom I love, what I hate. I no longer admire the impregnable infrastructure that make their lives work so well for them.

These admissions force me to disclose yet one more, the most damning of all: I have failed in the quest which brought me to

Lovelady. I must accept that the town will not, cannot be my home, and for the most self-limiting reason: because I *wish* to remain apart from it, need to feel separate, enjoy some self-serving distinction that in the end defeats me, limits me.

In short, I am caught in a paradox of my own making. Determined to remain a minority and yet miserable belonging to one, I fall back on a peevish list of reasons to explain why I find myself in this position: any Fox News program being televised during a meal; almost any speech by local or state Republican politicians; any amused (or angry) jokes about welfare mothers; any stories about rote abuse of food stamps; any blanket statements about welfare checks; any automatic stamp of approval of military personnel or military ceremonies; any automatic presumption about blacks (for example, they all litter); any megaphoned patriotism; any self-serving dismissal of health care as a "right"; any uninformed derision of the word "socialism"; any Biblical explanations of natural law.

And yet. The people who inspire this list are the same people who have, for the last ten years, made me dinner when I had kidney stones, created a thoughtful memorial service for my mother, taken me to the emergency room at 4 a.m., showed me as many kindnesses as stars in the sky. What mystery of the human spirit allows them to combine these examples of Christian charity while owning so many un-Christian and uncharitable opinions and behaviors? Why, for instance, does their unqualified hatred of abortion outweigh, for me, the pound cakes they have brought me on so many birthdays?

Clearly, I am as perplexed as I was when I arrived in my little town. Clearly, I will need to move somewhere more affirming of my own biases, where I can create my own little ghetto. And just as clearly, I acknowledge how much I would have preferred a different outcome.

But that outcome is as inevitable as one other fact: the time has arrived to say good-bye to my little town and its citizens. I can feel the catch in my throat already. So long, Lovelady. Farewell, Mr. Nielsen. Till then, Tiny Thompson and Mary Margaret and Cassie. Glad to have met you, Reverend Dan, Pat and Bill, Florence, Rusty, Mr. Thomas. What we had, my ill-fated experiment so full of the best intentions, is already receding into history. But, as it disappears, please know this: you have left an ineffable mark on one man's heart, an imprint that runs deep, even as I write this, in another town, in another country.

Bibliography

Agee, James, and Walker Evans. *Let Us Now Praise Famous Men*. Ballantine Books: 1939.

Ayers, Edward L. and Bradley C. Mittendorf. *The Oxford Book of the American South: Testimony, Memory, and Fiction*. Oxford University Press: 1997.

Bell, Daniel. *The End of Ideology: On the Exhaustion of Political Ideas in the Fifties*. Harvard University Press: 1960

Brown, Mary Ward. *It Wasn't All Dancing: And Other Stories*. University of Alabama Press: 2002.

Byron, Lord. *Lord Byron: The Major Works*. Oxford's World Classics: 2008.

Cash, W. J. *The Mind of the South*. Alfred A. Knopf: 1941.

Chesnut, Mary Boykin. *A Diary from Dixie*. Harvard University Press: 1980.

Chicago Statement on Biblical Inerrancy. International Council on Bible Inerrancy: 1978.

Coombs, Edith. *America Visited: Famous Travelers Report on the United States in the 18th and 19th Centuries*. The Book League of America: 1940.

Decter, Midge. *Always Right: Selected Writings of Midge Decter*. Heritage Foundation: 2002.

Didion, Joan. "On Keeping a Notebook." *Slouching Toward Bethlehem*. Macmillan: 1968.

Duncan, Andy. *Alabama Curiosities*. Globe Pequot: 2008.

Faulkner, William. *Absalom, Absalom!* Random House: 1936.

Goethe, J. W. Von. *The Sorrow of Young Werther*. Dover Thrift Editions: 2002.

Goffman, Erving. *The Presentation of Self in Everyday Life*. Doubleday: 1959.

Grant, Richard. *Dispatches from Pluto: Lost and Found in the Mississippi Delta*. Simon and Schuster: 2015.

Harris, W. Stuart *A History of Perry County, Vols. I and II*. W. Stuart Harris: 1991.

Isenberg, Nancy. *White Trash: The 400-Year Untold History of Class in America*. Penguin: 2016.

Kincaid, Jamaica. *A Small Place*. Farrar, Straus, Giroux: 2000.

Lewis, Sinclair. *Main Street*. Harcourt, Brace, and Howe: 1920.

Merwin, W. S. *The Collected Poems of W. S. Merwin*. Library of America: 2013.

Murakami, Haruki. *Blind Willow, Sleeping Woman*. Harvill Secker: 2006.

Naipaul, V. S. *A Turn in the South*. Random House: 1989.

O'Connor, Flannery. *The Complete Stories of Flannery O'Connor*. Farrar, Straus, Giroux: 1971.

Ouyang, Helen. "Where Health Care Won't Go." *Harper's Magazine*, June 2017.

Percy, Walker. *Signposts in a Strange Land*. Farrar, Straus and Giroux: 1991.

Percy, William Alexander. *Lanterns on the Levee: Recollections of a Planter's Son*. Alfred A. Knopf: 1941.

Preston, John. *Hometowns: Gay Men Write about Where They Belong*. Plume: 1991.

Pym, Barbara. *Excellent Women*. Penguin Classics: 1962.

Rodriguez, Richard. "Late Victorians." *Harper's Magazine*. October 1990.

Sabol, Blair. "A Yankee Pilgrim in the Old South." *New York Times Magazine*: April 24, 1977.

Woodward, Colin. *American Nations*. Viking: 2011.

Wordsworth, William. *The Poetical Works of William Wordsworth*. Oxford University Press: 1941.

Yeats, William Butler. *The Celtic Twilight: Fairie and Folklore*. Dover Publications: 1893.